ENDORSEMENTS

Pastor Danny Diaz is one of God's true generals. In *A Life Designed by God*, he dares to challenge the reader out of passivity and into purpose! Using candid, real-life examples, Pastor Diaz makes this message resoundingly clear—God has already deposited within you all that you will ever need to walk out your destiny. You were engineered to be a success!

—Pastor Paula White
Church without Walls International

At the very moment we are conceived, God has a plan and a purpose for our lives. In his book, *A Life Designed by God*, Pastor Danny Diaz helps us to become aware of the potential greatness that is in each and every one of us. This book will help us discover who we were meant to be and walk in the calling and anointing that God alone has for us.

—Dr. Ron Kenoly
Ron Kenoly Ministries

Danny Diaz offers a clear and promising pathway to bounce back, take on new strengths, and, by faith, shape new seasons of life. Watch as your inherent destiny from God emerges in greater ways, as your path unfolds as a shining light. Thanks, Pastor Danny, for showing us how to build a bridge between time and eternity, hope and faith, and to get us from where we are now to where God calls us to be!

—*Dr. Mark J. Chironna*
The Master's Touch International Church

Danny Diaz is an encourager. His latest book, *A Life Designed by God*, takes you to the next level in knowing and realizing the plans and purposes God has for your life. I highly endorse this book as a "must have" in the devotional library of every Christian leader!

—*Michael McKinney, Ph.D.*
President, Promise Christian University, Pasadena, CA

A Life Designed by GOD

A Life Designed by GOD

Discovering Who *You* Were Meant to Be

Danny Diaz

WHITAKER
HOUSE

A LIFE DESIGNED BY GOD:
Discovering Who You Were Meant to Be

For speaking engagements, please contact Danny Diaz at:
Victorious Living Christian Center
3427-A Pomona Blvd.
Pomona, California 91768
www.dannydiaz.com

ISBN-13: 978-0-88368-621-8
ISBN: 0-88368-621-X
Printed in the United States of America
© 2007 by Danny Diaz

1030 Hunt Valley Circle
New Kensington, PA 15068
www.whitakerhouse.com

Library of Congress Cataloging-in-Publication Data

Diaz, Danny, 1950–
A life designed by God : discovering who you were meant to be / Danny Diaz.
p. cm.
Summary: "By leaving mistakes in the past and focusing on the future that God has designed for them, believers may step into a life of infinite possibilities"—Provided by publisher.
ISBN-13: 978-0-88368-621-8 (trade pbk. : alk. paper)
ISBN-10: 0-88368-621-X (trade pbk. : alk. paper) 1. Christian life. I. Title.
BV4501.3.D53 2007
248.4—dc22 2006100115

1 2 3 4 5 6 7 8 9 10 11 12 ᴜᴜ 15 14 13 12 11 10 09 08 07

DEDICATION

I dedicate this book to my wonderful wife, Yolanda, for her unfailing love, encouragement, and support.

To my parents, Daniel and Velia Diaz, for always loving and believing in me.

To my loving daughter, Yvette, and her husband, Don, who faithfully labor with me in the ministry.

To my son, Daniel, and his wife, Jennifer, for the blessing they are to my life.

To my grandchildren, Timothy and Jessica, for the inspiration they bring into my life.

To my sister, Rev. Irma Diaz, for her prayers and encouragement.

Last, but not least, to my Lord and Savior, Jesus Christ, the real author of this book!

Acknowledgments

With my heartfelt thanks:

- To Matt and Laurie Crouch, for so wonderfully producing the TBN special on which this book is based.

- To Dr. Paul and Jan Crouch, for setting in place their worldwide network, TBN, enabling this message to be seen and heard throughout the world.

- To Reverend Dorise Vance, for her dedication, prayers, and support, not only in this project but throughout my twenty years of ministry.

- To my beloved congregation at Victorious Living Christian Center, for faithfully inspiring me and pulling out what God has deposited in me for the now of times.

- To Bishop George G. Bloomer, for having the confidence in my call to write.

- To Kimberly Meadows, for her many hours of hard work on this project.

- To Pastor Paula White, for her encouragement.

- To Dr. Mark Chironna, my dear friend, who is always available to affirm and strengthen me.

- To my friend Dr. Ron Kenoly, for his powerful endorsement of this book.

- To Dr. Michael McKinney for his friendship, his ongoing support, and his wonderful endorsement of this book.

CONTENTS

INTRODUCTION

B elieve it or not, regardless of your present situation, you were created with a destiny: to fulfill a God-ordained and God-designed purpose. Unfortunately, for too many of us, the circumstances of life often seem to force us to surrender to the trials of life, driving us into the corner of mediocrity, when all the while, we have a Father who wants us to experience a life that's full and overflowing with blessing and meaning.

My desire is that you would know there is a God who has designed a great life for you. Before the foundation of the world, in the mind of the Sovereign One, you were created with destiny and purpose residing within you. No longer must you live beneath your privilege, expecting little from life and receiving even less. If your vision has been clouded by the cares of this world and you've ceased to move toward your destiny, be encouraged.

This book will help you to understand that you were not placed upon this earth by happenstance, but for a purpose. You will learn that your position in Christ is much greater than your present circumstance might reflect. Many great men and women of the Bible were faced with the stigma of defeat until the miraculous hand of God opened their spiritual eyes to reveal who they really were and why they were created. It is vitally important to recognize your spiritual authority and purpose in the kingdom. It is so important that the enemy will often send all manner of distractions to steer you toward an alternate destination—his wasteland of defeat.

I know that wasteland. Much of my life was aimlessly void of knowing my true purpose and destiny. I wasted away in alcoholism, almost lost my family, and watched hopelessly as life seemed to pass me by, leaving the wreckage of my existence in its wake. That is, until the Lord sent His Word to my rescue! I soon learned that even though I had only limited knowledge of who He truly is as a person, God knew me from the foundation of the world. God had recorded every day of my life in His book. I began to understand that there was more to my life than what I'd been experiencing, and I looked forward to walking in the newness of life that God has promised. I began to see the bigger picture of God's purpose for my life, and today I am a living witness of His re-creative power!

Jeremiah 1:5 says, *"Before I formed you in the womb I knew you; before you were born I sanctified you."* There is nothing about you that is a surprise to God. He knew about the trials you would face, but He also knew that one day He would deliver you and propel you into your purpose—if you would only choose to walk in this new life. Let's find out the type of life God has designed on your behalf before the foundation of the world!

—Pastor Danny Diaz

CHAPTER ONE

YOUR DAYS ARE WRITTEN

YOUR DAYS ARE WRITTEN

*Your eyes saw my substance, being yet
unformed. And in Your book they all were
written, the days fashioned for me,
when as yet there were none of them.*
—Psalm 139:16

Before you ever came into existence, God had a design for your life. As the psalm above so eloquently states, your days were written in eternity by the Author and Finisher of all things. Therefore, nothing you go through comes as a shock to God. There is no enticing snare of the devil for which God has not already made provision.

During very strenuous times, you may find yourself wandering about as one who has no hope, but when you realize your incredible significance in the eyes of God, you will receive a newfound faith to press on toward your higher calling in Christ Jesus. He is King over your life, which means that He desires to rule over every problem and troubling situation that you will ever face.

Days have been ordained on your behalf. Certainly, you still have choices and free will, and there may be a variety of ways in which your design is realized, but you need to choose to walk in His design—not in your own. It is when we grasp this enormous reality that we are able to embrace a peace that surpasses all understanding, even when our trials seem too much to bear.

> *No temptation has overtaken you except such as is common to man; but God is faithful, who will not allow you to be tempted beyond what you are able, but with the temptation will also make the way of escape, that you may be able to bear it.* (1 Corinthians 10:13)

There is a strength within that you have not yet experienced. Because you are His creation, fashioned in His image, He knows your limitations, and it is by His power that you are able to thrive.

REGARDLESS OF HOW YOU FEEL ABOUT YOUR PRESENT CIRCUMSTANCES, THE LORD KNEW YOU AND PLANNED YOUR DESTINY BEFORE CREATION.

"Jesus Christ [the living Word that was made flesh] *is the same yesterday, today, and forever"* (Hebrews 13:8). In Him *"there is no variation or shadow of turning"* (James 1:17). He was before all things and created all things. (See Colossians 1:16–17.) Regardless of how you feel about your present circumstances, the Lord knew you and planned your destiny before creation. *"You formed my inward parts; You covered me in my mother's womb"* (Psalm 139:13). He knows the end from

the beginning and the beginning from the end. (See Revelation 1:8.)

Jeremiah 29:11 says, *"For I know the thoughts that I think toward you, says the* L ORD, *thoughts of peace and not of evil, to give you a future and a hope."* God has great expectation in His heart concerning you and your life. He believes in you even if you've never believed in yourself and knows, with all His sovereign wisdom, that you *can* do that for which He designed you. He gives you the potential to finish the course, and He knows that, through His Son Jesus Christ, you can make it all the way.

> *For You formed my inward parts; You covered me in my mother's womb. I will praise You, for I am fearfully and wonderfully made; marvelous are Your works, and that my soul knows very well. My frame was not hidden from You, when I was made in secret, and skillfully wrought in the lowest parts of the earth. Your eyes saw my substance, being yet unformed. And in Your book they all were written, the days fashioned for me, when as yet there were none of them. How precious also are Your thoughts to me, O God! How great is the sum of them!*
>
> (Psalm 139:13–17)

To the finite, limited vision of man, your endeavor may seem impossible to accomplish, but as Jesus once said, *"With men it is impossible, but not with God; for with God all things are possible"* (Mark 10:27).

Remember, God is the Creator, and He has commanded you, His creation, to subdue the earth:

Then God blessed them [His creation], *and God said to them, "Be fruitful and multiply; fill the earth and subdue it; have dominion over the fish of the sea, over the birds of the air, and over every living thing that moves on the earth."*

(Genesis 1:28)

Every adversity you will ever face has already been provided for, but you must choose to enforce what Jesus has done and overcome the work of the devil that attempts to hinder God's design. He is the Creator; you're the enforcer. You're called to be an imitator of God. You are called to your promised land, not to the land of mediocrity. We serve a God who is more than enough! So, don't compromise His greatness by settling for marginal progress and average thinking.

THE LAND OF MEDIOCRITY

Picture, if you will, the land of Mediocrity. Perhaps it is a place where you have chosen to make your home. But this land does not exist in isolation. There are other lands around that have left their influence on Mediocrity.

COMPROMISE

Just to the north is the land of Compromise. Compromise entices you to conform to the ideologies of the world's standards rather than allowing your situation to conform to the Word of God.

Compromise means many things. Obviously, to compromise your walk would be to walk in sin. But a much more subtle form of compromise is when you find yourself settling for less than what God has designed for your life. The righteousness of God bestows many blessings on the body of Christ on a daily basis. But many within the body continue to compromise those blessings right out of their lives. Too often, they invent excuses for giving in to compromise:

- ✓ "Well, I guess that's not what God wanted for my life."
- ✓ "It will be easier to do this instead."
- ✓ "I'm desperate, so I'll just have to settle for whatever comes my way."

Sound familiar? I believe that Compromise is the leading cause of mediocrity. Therefore, we must stand up against compromised thinking and know, in the name of Jesus, that God has designed a plan and purpose for our lives. Refuse to compromise. Refuse to live life in the past. Refuse to give in.

INDECISION AND CONFUSION

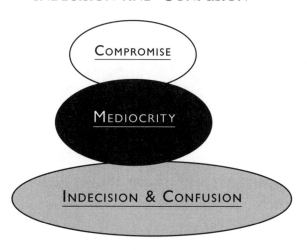

If Mediocrity is a land bordered on the north by compromise, then the land to the south would be Indecision and Confusion. This is a place that will hold you back, leaving you spinning your wheels as you try to decide whether to step out or stand still. Fortunately, we can rely on God's Word that He does not want us to stay there long. In fact, He can lead us out. *"For God is not the author of confusion"* (1 Corinthians 14:33). *"I will instruct you and teach you in the way you should go; I will guide you with My eye"* (Psalm 32:8). It will take a conscious decision and a clear vision to discover the kind of life that God has designed on your behalf. Indecision and confusion bring the progress of the body of Christ to a grinding halt.

Early in the ministry, I was in Texas ministering the Word, and I told the people that whatever we ask according to God's will, He has promised us we will receive. (See John 16:23.) I assured them that this is the confidence that we have in Him—that if we ask, He hears us; and if He hears us, He will give us the petitions we have asked for. (See 1 John 5:14.) I preached this message with zest and with the fervor of anticipation. It was a very hot and humid day, and many people lined up for prayer. On that day, I first began to operate in my prophetic spiritual gift—and according to God's design for my life.

Since that day, the Lord has continued to bless me with the ability to operate in the prophetic gifts. When I pray for people, I pray according to a word of knowledge, of wisdom, and of prophecy. I can't explain it, but I always seem to know what I need to say. These prophetic gifts of God are actively operating in my life. That is why I was shocked when I prayed for one particular man.

> INDECISION AND CONFUSION BRING THE PROGRESS OF THE BODY OF CHRIST TO A GRINDING HALT.

I asked him, "What would you like me to pray for?"

"Well," he said, "I need a new job because I don't make enough money at my present one."

I explained to him, "Whatever you ask in His name, He will do." I began to pray, "Father, in the name of Jesus...." I prayed so eloquently, crossing every "t" and dotting every "i."

Suddenly, he stopped me and said, "Wait a minute. Actually I make quite a bit of money. The reason I need a new job is not because of the money, but because I need to be able to do something for Jesus. Right now, I can't do anything. I can't witness for Him. I can't do anything or be of any use to Jesus on this job."

"Fine," I said. "You don't need a new job for that; we'll ask God to open the door for you so you can witness on the job."

Again I began to pray, "In Jesus' name, open the door for him to be a witness for You and to show people the love that You have set forth on their behalf." Again he stopped me.

"No," he said. "That's not the reason. I talk to people all day, and I get to witness all the time."

"Well," I said, "why do you think you need a new job?"

He responded, "It's the people that I work for. They're not believers. They're hard to work for and hard to get along with."

I offered him some advice, "You don't need to get a new job. God can tenderize their hearts and bring them to the right side. He can also make them very nice to you. Let's pray. 'Father, in the name of Jesus….'"

"Hold on a minute," he interrupted. "I cannot be a false witness against my neighbor. Actually my bosses are pretty nice. Last summer they loaned me their boat for my vacation."

Growing frustrated, I simply looked at him and said, "Come out, in Jesus' name!"

Here was a guy who was plagued with indecision and confusion. Together, we prayed that the Lord would take those spirits away from him. "Lord, You are not the author of confusion. Take this spirit of constant indecision away from this man, causing him to change his mind, right now!"

After praying, I said to him, "Brother, tell me your name so that when the Lord brings you to my consciousness, I'll be able to pray for you."

He answered, "My name's Bill."

I said, "Well, Bill, God bless you and congratulations."

Before turning and walking away, he said, "Wait a minute, my name's William. My parents always call me William."

It just killed me. There I was, praying with all my might, and this guy still couldn't even decide what his own name was.

You may think this was merely a rather humorous encounter in ministry, but for me it became a sober reminder of the kind of dangerous stronghold the evil one can have in a believer's life. It was a learning experience that enhanced my ability to minister to the needs of others who were suffering from these same curses of compromise and indecision.

VIEWING THE PAST AS THE PRESENT

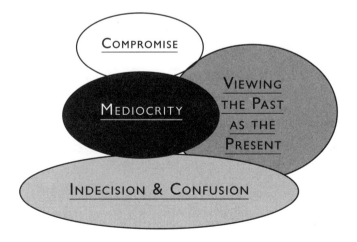

All right, let's go back to our map of the land of Mediocrity. Just to the east lies a land I call Viewing the Past as the Present. Despite its rather long and awkward name, this place is very real.

One night, as I walked into my backyard to relax, I began to ponder the awesomeness of God and His concern for our every need and desire. As the sun began to set beyond the mountainous terrain, I stared at the hills and noticed the trees in a way I'd never seen them before. Joy began to permeate my heart as I reflected on the detailed thoughts of God and how He'd blessed me with the ability to enjoy this magnificent scenery from the comforts of my own backyard. The trees displayed their beauty, the rolling hills stood as a picture-perfect landscape, and the glowing stars began to show forth their glory against the darkening sky.

I suddenly began to meditate on the meticulous detail that the Father used to create the universe.

> *Then God said, "Let there be lights in the firmament of the heavens to divide the day from the night; and let them be for signs and seasons, and for days and years; and let them be for lights in the firmament of the heavens to give light on the earth"; and it was so. Then God made two great lights: the greater light to rule the day, and the lesser light to rule the night. He made the stars also. God set them in the firmament of the heavens to give light on the earth, and to rule over the day and over the night, and to divide the light from the darkness. And God saw that it was good.*
>
> (Genesis 1:14–18)

I realized that nothing exists without the hand of God; all things were created by Him and for Him, and He alone holds it all together.

> He [Jesus] *is the image of the invisible God, the firstborn over all creation. For by him all things were created: things in heaven and on earth, visible and invisible, whether thrones or powers or rulers or authorities; all things were created by him and for him. He is before all things,* **and in him all things hold together.**
>
> (Colossians 1:15–17 NIV, emphasis added)

I started thinking about the vastness of His mighty and sovereign abilities. But as I stared up into that evening sky, I began to realize that when we look at the evening sky, we are not seeing things as they are—we are actually seeing things as they were. Let me explain.

According to NASA, the light of the nearest star, with the exception of the sun, takes just over four years to reach the earth. Therefore, the next time you gaze up into the night sky, you are actually seeing what that star looked like four years ago, not what it looks like today. You are literally viewing the past in the present.

> TOO MANY PEOPLE ALLOW THE PAIN, DEFEAT, AND NEGATIVE ATTITUDES OF THE PAST TO DEFINE THEIR PRESENT LIVES, THEREBY LETTING YESTERDAY'S FAILURES HINDER THEIR ABILITY TO RECEIVE GOD'S BLESSINGS TODAY.

As I was lying there stargazing in my backyard, the Lord revealed to me a frequent problem in the body of Christ: too many people are stuck because they are viewing their past as the present. They are allowing the pain, defeat, and negative attitudes of the past to define their present lives, thereby allowing yesterday's failures to hinder their ability to receive God's blessings today. Surprisingly enough, some are even allowing past successes to stand in their way of God's present-day blessings.

It's like the pastor who tells you over and over about his ministry—that in 1992, over 15,000 souls were saved. But if you ask him what he has been doing for the Lord since that time, he answers, "Well, in 1992 we had all these people who came to the Lord." But what is he doing now? His past success is actually holding him back because he's looking at the present in light of the past. He's not able to see the light of today because the brightness of the light of the past has blinded his present sight.

People who allow past successes to hinder their future are living according to a light that came forth years ago. They are allowing the past to hold them back from what God has designed for their lives before the foundation of the world.

Dwelling on the past and allowing it to dictate and determine your present direction will lead you right back to the state of mediocrity every time. This is not to say that you must completely ignore your past. Sometimes you have to work through the events of your past in order to gain the victory so that you can move forward to see the future in the present. We must learn the lessons from our past but not allow it to guide our future steps.

A LACK OF VISION

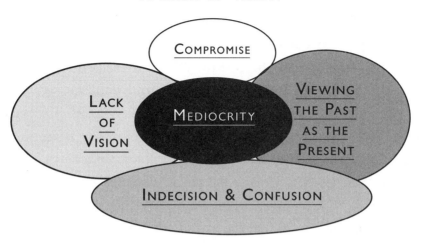

The final bordering territory to Mediocrity is a land called A Lack of Vision—actually the inability to view the future in the present. God says, *"Where there is no vision, the people perish"* (Proverbs 29:18). A lack of vision—viewing a future direction in the present—destroys the body of Christ. Far too often, greatness and blessings have gone down the proverbial drain because people are so focused on their past they completely miss out on God's vision for their future.

WALKING OUT THE WORD

The more time you spend viewing your past in the present, the longer you're going to remain stagnant because you are continuing to stare at the same old thing. The only way to create some inertia and move from where you are camped is to discover God's incredible designs for your life. You will not hear it blasted over some loudspeaker. The only way I know of to find it is to "walk out" God's Word. And as you walk out the Word—applying His concepts to your daily life—God will begin to uncover the many treasures that He has prepared just for you.

In order to walk out this path, however, you must have faith and know with all your heart that there is not one thing lacking from your life. Anytime you find yourself wavering or discouraged, remind yourself of this vitally important fact: "God has provided *all* that I need. Nothing is missing." It is God *"who is able to do exceedingly abundantly above all that we ask or think, according to the power that works in us"* (Ephesians 3:20). *"Exceedingly abundantly."* I love that. According to *Merrian-Webster's Dictionary, a*bundant means "a great plenty, amply supplied," and *exceedingly* means "to an extreme degree." That means abundance, more than we could ever need!

> **WHEN THE ENEMY CONFRONTS YOU, YOU NEED TO REMIND HIM THAT YOUR DAYS HAVE BEEN DESIGNED BY THE AUTHOR AND FINISHER OF ALL THINGS.**

In Christ we become new creations: *"If anyone is in Christ, he is a new creation; old things have passed away; behold, all things have become new"* (2 Corinthians 5:17). When you look at the evening sky, you are seeing nothing but a reflection of the past—what used to be. Jesus has redeemed you, and now God wants you to begin to see your future in the present.

We know from Scripture that *"faith is the substance of things hoped for, the evidence of things not seen"* (Hebrews 11:1). Therefore, when the enemy confronts you, you need to remind him that your days have been preordained, designed by the Author and Finisher of all things. No longer do you need to settle for mediocrity. No longer must you endure the devil's distractions and attacks on the blessing and purpose that God has designed for your future.

JESUS SHOWED US HOW

When Jesus first began His ministry, He waded into the Jordan River where John the Baptist was busy baptizing people. John immediately felt His presence, looked up and said, *"I need to be baptized by you, and do you come to me?"* (Matthew 3:14 NIV). Jesus reminded John, *"Let it be so now; it is proper for us to do this to fulfill all righteousness"* (verse 15 NIV). This day, this baptism, was part of God's design for Jesus' life. John obeyed and baptized Jesus. Scripture says,

> *As soon as Jesus was baptized, he went up out of the water. At that moment heaven was opened, and he saw the Spirit of God descending like a dove and lighting on him. And a voice from heaven said, "This is my Son, whom I love; with him I am well pleased."* (Matthew 3:16–17 NIV)

Recognizing the meaning of this moment, John acknowledged that God's design for his life was being realized:

> *Look, the Lamb of God, who takes away the sin of the world! This is the one I meant when I said, "A man who comes after me has surpassed me because he was before me." I myself did not know him, but the reason I came baptizing with water was that he might be revealed to Israel.* (John 1:29–31)

After Jesus' baptism, along came the devil with a different plan. He knew that, since Jesus was fully human, He felt hunger. Satan simply said, *"If You are the Son of God, command that these stones become bread"* (Matthew 4:3). Jesus replied with the Word of God, *"It is written, 'Man shall not live by bread alone, but by every word that proceeds from the mouth of God'"* (verse 4). Jesus was basically saying, "Why should I turn the rocks into bread? I am the Bread." Two more times, Satan came at Jesus with different plans, but each time Jesus addressed him by saying the words, *"It is written."* (See verses 7, 10.) Satan was defeated by what had already been written by the hand of God and was forced to flee.

God has designed a purpose for you and has given you the potential to complete that design. He has blessed you with everything you need to finish. The devil's plan, as it was with Jesus, is to take it from you—to abolish what God has done and keep you from fulfilling your design. Every time Satan rears his head, you simply need to remind him, "I must fulfill all righteousness. I'm a believer priest under the Father through the blood of the Son, an heir of God and a joint heir with Christ. Get behind me, Satan, because my life has a purpose and design from God. In God's Word *'they all were written, the days fashioned for me'* (Psalm 139:16)."

TRIP OVER GOD'S PURPOSE

God didn't bring you this far to leave you. Whatever He starts, He finishes. Each day, as you walk out His Word, you can't help but trip over God's purpose for your life. But if you lie around watching television, surfing the Internet, or otherwise wasting countless hours when God calls you and tries to speak to you, then you will continue to miss His revelation.

You must choose to embrace the things that God has designed for your life. Some folks complain, "I just can't hear God's voice. I don't know what His intention is for my life." As you renew your mind according to the Word of God, you begin to transform and prove the good, acceptable purpose and intent that God has for your life. (See Romans 12:2.) Just walk the day through in faith, and even when it seems as if nothing is taking place in the natural, continue on the path that God has chosen and embrace the outcome of every step you take. Each day that you fulfill propels you into the next day, and as you walk through each day in faith, more of God's purpose will begin to unfold. *"Those who wait on the LORD shall renew their strength; they shall mount up with wings like eagles, they shall run and not be weary, they shall walk and not faint"* (Isaiah 40:31). If you wait upon God and His purposes, and do not grow weary, you will be empowered to fulfill the designs that God has for your life.

> GOD DIDN'T BRING YOU THIS FAR TO LEAVE YOU. WHATEVER HE STARTS, HE FINISHES.

If you don't learn to see the future in the present, you will be significantly hindered. You have to know what God says about you, even when it appears that the opposite is occurring in the natural. You have to be aware and alert to God's design. Do you realize that you could be searching for something all your life that was always there, staring you right in the face? You must be aware of God's promises for your life:

Christ has redeemed us from the curse of the law.

(Galatians 3:13)

33

If you are Christ's, then you are Abraham's seed, and heirs according to the promise. (Galatians 3:29)

Submit to God. Resist the devil and he will flee from you. (James 4:7)

With a spiritual awareness and enlightenment of who you are, you will be better able to *"press toward the mark for the prize of the high calling of God"* (Philippians 3:14 KJV).

Each of us has a "promised land" that God wants to lead us into, but what carried you through the wilderness will not get you into the promise. For that, you must move from the human-driven, conditional, logical ways of doing things and into a state of walking in faith according to God's Word. When you walk in faith, however, don't rely on ritual or formalism to empower you; rather, rely on God's revelation. You need to know by revelation what God has given you. By the power of the anointing, *"in all your ways acknowledge Him, and He shall direct your paths"* (Proverbs 3:6). He's not going to send you where you're not supposed to be. When you move the mountain by revelation, by the spirit of faith, it is buried in the sea, never to rise again.

SPRINGBOARD INTO YOUR FUTURE

Can you imagine if Mary Magdalene had viewed the past in the present? She wouldn't have believed that she could possibly reach out and touch the Lord. How could she go to the tomb to anoint His body? Yet she was able to use her past as a springboard into her future by not viewing the past in the present, but by beholding all that she had become by the power of God. Mary Magdalene was the first human being to lay eyes on the risen Christ. That day was a part of her purpose. She was in the process of becoming the woman that God designed her to be, and she acted accordingly, refusing to view the past in the present and rejecting a life of mediocrity.

The only way you're going to realize the fullness of God's design for your life is to renew your mind according to His vision and according to His Word. When you get there, you'll find yourself in the Scriptures, and no longer will they be words on a page or ancient stories. You'll begin to see your future in those pages. No longer will you be so concerned with the mistakes that you've made in the past. No longer will you allow them to stagnate your growth. You will begin to use them as valuable learning experiences that will help to springboard you toward your future, allowing your future to determine your present course.

> TO GET INTO YOUR PROMISED LAND, YOU NEED TO MOVE FROM THE HUMAN-DRIVEN, CONDITIONAL, LOGICAL WAYS OF DOING THINGS AND INTO A STATE OF WALKING IN FAITH ACCORDING TO GOD'S WORD.

As we read in Jeremiah 1:5, before God formed you in your mother's womb, He already knew you. But the *you* He knew was more than just the physical "you"; it was also a purpose and destiny that He designed for you to specifically fulfill. You are not an accident. From eternity past He foreknew you, and whom He foreknew, He predestined; whom He predestined, He called; whom He called, He justified; and whom He justified, He glorified. (See Romans 8:29–30.) *"What then shall we say to these things* [all the adversity that the enemy continues to toss in our path]? *If God is for us, who can be against us?"* (Romans 8:31). Your life has a design and a purpose. Nothing can defeat that design—except you.

Jesus has shown us how to walk in purpose and design. Now it's your turn. Let's press on and learn how to possess God's promises and claim our place of authority in Him.

WHATEVER YOU WALK ON WILL BE YOURS

WHATEVER YOU WALK ON WILL BE YOURS: WALKING OUT YOUR DESIGN

Moses My servant is dead. Now therefore, arise, go over this Jordan, you and all this people, to the land which I am giving to them; the children of Israel. Every place that the sole of your foot will tread upon I have given you.
—Joshua 1:2–3

Four questions are often asked by believers throughout the body of Christ:

- Who am I?
- Where did I come from?
- Why am I here?
- Where am I going?

WHO AM I?

This is a question of personal identity. Too often, many of those within the church who have a great destiny in Christ allow the world to define them instead of allowing the Holy Spirit to reveal who they truly are.

In Matthew, in the middle of a story about sparrows, Jesus makes an incredible statement: *"The very hairs of your head are all numbered"* (Matthew 10:30). Do you still think you are an accident? An afterthought of the Almighty? Jesus says that God has numbered every hair on your head. You are an individual, uniquely crafted according to God's wonderful plan. By the blood of Jesus Christ, you are the apple of His eye.

WHERE DID I COME FROM?

This is a question regarding personal history. In the last chapter, we learned that we must not view the past in the present; rather, we must learn to see the future in the present in order to proceed along the proper journey to fulfill the plans that God has for us. Therefore, you need to know that your past does not define where you are today; your future must determine where you are. God has given you a great future, and the sooner you begin to walk according to who He has made you, the sooner you'll begin to walk in your purpose and destiny. But remember, success is not a destination—it's a journey of discovery.

SUCCESS IS NOT A DESTINATION—IT'S A JOURNEY OF DISCOVERY.

The apostle Paul knew that God's destiny and design was a journey. Paul knew his goal: *"That I may know Him* [Jesus] *and the power of His resurrection, and the fellowship of His sufferings, being conformed to His death"* (Philippians 3:10). Paul knew, even late in life, that his purpose and design were still being worked out: *"Not that I have already attained, or am already perfected"* (verse 12).

If I were thrown in prison, I daresay that I might feel the temptation to give up. But Paul knew the path he had to walk, not sitting still in mediocrity or dwelling on his past:

> *I press on, that I may lay hold of that for which Christ Jesus has also laid hold of me. Brethren, I do not count myself to have apprehended; but one thing I do, forgetting those things which are behind and reaching forward to those things which are ahead, I press toward the goal for the prize of the upward call of God in Christ Jesus.* (Philippians 3:12–14)

Every step you take along the way is progress, but you must abide in Him as you make that progress.

WHY AM I HERE?

Everyone on this planet longs for a sense of purpose. People everywhere want to have a sense of why they exist. We all have a desire to feel needed and useful. When people lose this sense of purpose, depression and discouragement can set in, which often leads to destructive, even suicidal, tendencies.

God's people are designed and created for a purpose. We must put our foot down, square off with the forces of evil, and let them know exactly what we believe and in whom we believe. We must remind them that the Lord has made us who we are and nothing can stop us. *"In all these things we are more than conquerors through Him who loved us"* (Romans 8:37).

Where Am I Going?

This question refers to destiny. Everyone from the White House to skid row has a destiny, and it's important for every individual within the body of Christ to realize that they're not here by accident or mistake. They are on this planet to accomplish their God-given design. Remember, in Jeremiah 1:5, the Lord said that before He formed you in your mother's womb He knew you. You may have come from your mother's womb physically, but spiritually you came from the womb of God's heart, and you're here for a purpose, equipped with a mighty destiny.

You are a child of destiny created with promise, but until these four questions are resolved within your heart and mind according to God's Word, you will not be able to walk through the doors of opportunity that He creates for you.

Possess the Land

According to Galatians 3:29, if you belong to Jesus, you are also Abraham's seed—heirs to God's promise to Israel. Just as the children of Israel had a land of promise, so does everyone who is in Christ today. Everyone who is in the family of God, adopted by the blood of the Lamb, is experiencing that land of promise to some degree.

> *After the death of Moses the servant of the Lord, it came to pass that the Lord spoke to Joshua the son of Nun, Moses'*

assistant, saying: "Moses My servant is dead. Now therefore, arise, go over this Jordan, you and all this people, to the land which I am giving to them; the children of Israel. Every place that the sole of your foot will tread upon I have given you, as I said to Moses."...Then Joshua commanded the officers of the people, saying, "Pass through the camp and command the people, saying, 'Prepare provisions for yourselves, for within three days you will cross over this Jordan, to go in to possess the land which the LORD your God is giving you to possess.'"   (Joshua 1:1–3, 10–11)

Because you are an heir to the promise, Scripture says that whatever you walk on will be yours. Every place that the sole of your foot shall tread upon belongs to you. If the Lord said it, it is settled; if He spoke it, He will bring it to pass.

GET OUT OF THE BOAT

In the gospel of Matthew, chapter fourteen, we are given an account of Jesus' ministry along with His disciples.

Jesus made His disciples get into the boat and go before Him to the other side, while He sent the multitudes away. And when He had sent the multitudes away, He went up on the mountain by Himself to pray.   (Matthew 14:22–23)

The disciples went to the boat and began their journey across the lake. Scripture says that in the fourth watch of the night, between 3:00 and 6:00 a.m., the boat began to struggle in a storm. So, Jesus went to them, but He didn't take a boat. He went out to their boat walking on the water!

When the disciples saw Him walking on the sea, they were troubled, saying, "It is a ghost!" And they cried out for fear. But immediately Jesus spoke to them, saying, "Be of good cheer! It is I; do not be afraid." And Peter answered Him and said, "Lord, if it is You, command me to come to You on the water." So He said, "Come." (Matthew 14:26–29)

It was then that Peter stepped out of the boat onto the *instability* of the water and began walking on the *stability* of the word that Jesus had spoken.

Sometimes in life, even though it makes no logical sense, you must get out of the boat and begin to walk on the truth that God has written about you. Just as Peter got out of that boat and, looking at Jesus, began to walk on the water, we too know that Scripture says we are to *"run with endurance the race that is set before us, looking unto Jesus, the author and finisher of our faith"* (Hebrews 12:1–2).

CONTRARY TO WHAT YOU MAY HAVE THOUGHT, IT IS POSSIBLE TO SINK EVEN WHEN JESUS IS IN YOUR MIDST.

As Peter walked on the instability of the water, in his periphery he began to notice just how unstable his situation was. In that moment, he made the crucial mistake of thinking about the waves beneath him and began to believe that they were greater than the Living Water that beckoned him forward. Suddenly, he began to sink, and then, he did what each of us tend to do when we begin to sink—cried, *"Lord, save me!"* (Matthew 14:30). Immediately, Jesus reached out, caught Peter, and they both walked back to the boat on the stability of "the Rock."

Contrary to what you may have thought, it is possible to sink even when Jesus is in your midst. The anointing of God is working on your behalf. He has given you the go-ahead, and it's now time to get out of the boat, but you must keep your eyes on Him and not the instability of your present situation.

WATER-WALKING

Water is unstable. Two things happen when you put something in water: it either floats or it sinks. Unless you're full of hot air or Styrofoam, you're going to sink. But the instability of the water is also the field from which you will reap your harvest. Within instability you will discover a stability that far surpasses every obstacle and hindrance. But you need to walk out, by faith, that which has been designed on your behalf. Then, truly, whatever you walk on will be yours.

> *Moses My servant is dead. Now therefore, arise, go over this Jordan, you and all this people, to the land which I am giving to them; the children of Israel. Every place that the sole of your foot will tread upon I have given you.*
>
> (Joshua 1:2–3)

As we return to this passage in Joshua, notice that the Lord God Almighty was introducing Joshua to the transition from foundational-faith to accomplishing-faith. He was reminding Israel that what got them through the wilderness would not get them into the land of promise. Moses was now dead. But God commanded them to *"arise."* This power that would deliver them into their land of promise was the same resurrection power that would be displayed at an empty tomb generations later. That same resurrection power is available to you. God is saying, "Arise! Walk! Enter your land of promise."

The past is behind you, but if it is continuing to hinder you, you must deal with it in order to move forward. Not until you deal with your situation will you be able to put it behind you and earnestly ask the Lord, "What is in the future, and what is Your will for my life?"

I beseech you therefore, brethren, by the mercies of God, that you present your bodies a living sacrifice, holy, acceptable to God, which is your reasonable service. And do not be conformed to this world, but be transformed by the renewing of your mind, that you may prove what is that good and acceptable and perfect will of God. (Romans 12:1–2)

It is vital not to conform to the world's system, but instead, to renew your mind, present your body as a living sacrifice, and allow the transforming, resurrection power of the Holy Spirit to perfect the *"good and acceptable and perfect will of God"* in your life.

MORE THAN ENOUGH

Often, we are swift to believe what God has done for those in the past, but we struggle to receive His personal Word concerning our individual destiny for today. It may not be difficult for us to believe that Jesus actually walked on the water, but when we consider how Peter pulled off this feat, our minds are boggled at his amazing faith. What we fail to remember is that Jesus was 100 percent man as well as 100 percent God, and that the wondrous works He performed were done as an anointed man. Peter was able to grasp this revelation of God's divinity and humanity, and it provoked his faith to step out of the boat and perform the impossible. He was able to defy the mortal laws of this world and step out onto the laws of faith. Peter was far from perfect, but he was bold enough to get out of the boat and walk on water.

> **SOMETIMES YOU MUST BE WILLING TO STEP OUT OF THE BOAT IN THE MIDDLE OF THE STORM AND WALK ON THE INSTABILITY OF YOUR FEARS.**

Sometimes you must be willing to step out of the boat in the middle of the storm and walk on the instability of your fears. Walking on all that God has promised you allows you all the foundation you will ever need to conquer the unconquerable and possess your promised land.

Just after God had delivered the children of Israel from slavery in Egypt through Moses, they wandered in the wilderness. Despite the miracle of their deliverance, they still doubted God's provision and complained to Moses,

> *Oh, that we had died by the hand of the LORD in the land of Egypt, when we sat by the pots of meat and when we ate bread to the full! For you have brought us out into this wilderness to kill this whole assembly with hunger.*
>
> (Exodus 16:3)

Hearing their complaints, God provided them with sustenance from heaven—bread (manna) in the morning, and quails in the evening. They couldn't store up the manna for the future though; it only lasted for a day. Thus, they were forced into a daily dependence upon the promised provision of God.

Still, their faith in God's provision wavered:

Why is it you have brought us up out of Egypt, to kill us and our children and our livestock with thirst?

(Exodus 17:3)

Once again, hearing their complaint, God provided them with water. Even though God's promises were continually within eyesight on a daily basis, the people still lost faith and failed to find the Promised Land.

Likewise, God has already provided you with everything that you will ever need to walk out your designed destiny. You won't get there, however, until you stop doubting God with your foundational-faith "manna mentality" and transition into an accomplishing-faith, "more-than-enough" revelation of who God truly is and who He has designed you to be.

> GOD HAS ALREADY PROVIDED YOU WITH EVERYTHING THAT YOU WILL EVER NEED TO WALK OUT YOUR DESIGNED DESTINY.

In Matthew 16, when Jesus entered Caesarea Philippi with His disciples, He stopped and began to talk with them. *"Who do men say that I, the Son of Man, am?"* (Matthew 16:13). They began to answer Him based upon what they had heard, *"Some say John the Baptist, some Elijah, and others Jeremiah or one of the prophets"* (verse 14). Jesus then addressed them by requesting a more personal response, *"But who do you say that I am?"* (verse 15). After a moment of silence,

Simon Peter took a stand and responded, *"You are the Christ, the Son of the living God"* (verse 16). At that point, Jesus acknowledged the presence of God through Simon Peter's response:

Blessed are you, Simon Bar-Jonah, for flesh and blood has not revealed this to you, but My Father who is in heaven. And I also say to you that you are Peter, and on this rock I will build My church, and the gates of Hades shall not prevail against it. And I will give you the keys of the kingdom of heaven, and whatever you bind on earth will be bound in heaven, and whatever you loose on earth will be loosed in heaven. (Matthew 16:17–19)

The exact translation of that is "whatsoever you shall bind on earth is already bound in heaven and whatsoever you shall loose on earth is already loosed in heaven." You must enforce and maintain what Jesus has already bound and loosed. Then, you can enter into your land of promise—your designed purpose. You were delivered from Egypt (the land of *lack*) into the wilderness (the land of *just enough*), and now you are traveling toward your promised land (the land of *more than enough*). But you will not discover this land of plenty by following the ritualistic road map of tradition. The only way you're going to set foot in it is by revelation.

> KNOW THAT YOU ARE ON A JOURNEY TO A GREAT PLACE OF DESTINY, A LAND YOU INHERITED AS HEIR TO GOD'S PROMISE TO ABRAHAM.

Know that you are on a journey to a great place of destiny, a land you inherited as heir to God's promise to Abraham.

49

God Almighty has given you authority over all *"the power of the enemy, and nothing shall by any means hurt you"* (Luke 10:19). He reminds you that every place that the sole of your feet tread upon, He has given to you. (See Joshua 1:3.) Get out of the boat and prophesy over your Jordan, the river guarding your promised land, and watch the waters part as His anointing leads you forward.

FAITH AND MOUNTAIN-MOVING POWER

God is admonishing you to walk out on what He has written on your behalf. Refuse to remain where you are, conquer all fear, and step out. Don't stay where you've been. Fear is a giant that continually tries to intimidate us into backing down and accepting defeat. *"For God has not given us a spirit of fear, but of power and of love and of a sound mind"* (2 Timothy 1:7).

We must program our minds and spiritual insight to see as God sees. God has more faith in us than we have in ourselves. When you dare to step out of the boat and onto the instability of this world, you'll find that you're more stable than you've ever been. Why? Because you'll be standing on the rock.

Over the past several years, I have seen a "victim mentality" taking over the body of Christ. It isn't a new thing; it was going on in the wilderness in Exodus where the nation of Israel wandered for forty years, looking for something that was always there.

Today, many saints of God continually make this same mistake, wandering around looking for something that has always been in front of them. All that you need has been prepared from the foundation of the world and lies within you.

If you go to church looking for something that isn't already in you, you're not going to get it.

Undoubtedly, storms will arise, but the Word of God assures us, *"These things I have spoken to you, that in Me you may have peace. In the world you will have tribulation; but be of good cheer, I have overcome the world"* (John 16:33).

Jesus also said,

Have faith in God. For assuredly, I say to you, whoever says to this mountain, "Be removed and be cast into the sea," and does not doubt in his heart, but believes that those things he says will be done, he will have whatever he says.

(Mark 11:22–23)

In the same way, you possess the power to cast tribulation (your mountain) into the sea, never to be recovered again. Your mountain-moving faith glorifies God. So when faced with an obstacle, view it as an opportunity to show forth His glory, magnitude, and power.

THE WALK OF FAITH INVOLVES TRUSTING GOD NO MATTER WHAT OUR NATURAL SIGHT AND CIRCUMSTANCES PRESENT.

The walk of faith involves trusting God no matter what our natural sight and circumstances present. The walk of faith enables a man to sit down with his family and say with surety, "Alright, we have no food in the pantry. There's no food in the cupboard. But we're going to pray. We're going to dress up and wash our hands for dinner, because God said that He would give us our daily bread." Then, at that moment, when they all sit down to dinner, a miracle is brewing on the other side of the door. Something takes place outside. They hear a knock, and as they open the door, someone stands there whom God has used to provide what they need for their dinner. Impossible, you say? Of course it is, in the natural. Otherwise it wouldn't be a miracle. When Jesus talked about the power of faith, He could have talked about moving a boulder or a tree or a house, but no, He went right for moving mountains. That's what a miracle is. That's what faith can do. It can walk on water, heal a cripple, raise the dead, and even move mountains. The walk of faith is believing in the face of adversity. The walk of faith is taking joy in the adversity; for you know that you have already overcome.

Conquer the Storm

One day, I was experiencing excruciating pain. I told my wife, Yolanda, "I can barely stand the pain." She responded, "God will never allow you to experience more than you can handle." My wife continually reminds me of the things that I preach. She reminds me what the Word of God says that I am and what the Lord has revealed to my heart. She's an anointed woman who's not intimidated by the devices of Satan. In the face of adversity, she wastes no time making excuses, but immediately stands on the Word of God. My wife has had to remind me several times to cast down the objects of intimidation and manipulation that attempt to hinder my progression toward the promises of God.

The mentality of blaming everybody else for where you are must be cast down and put under your feet. Stop the blame game and begin to press toward the mark for the prize of your high calling. (See Philippians 3:14.) And when the storm begins to brew, just roll up your sleeves and remind the devil, "I am more than a conqueror (see Romans 8:37) through the blood of Jesus Christ, and whatever I walk upon will be mine." Learn to declare what God has already declared on your behalf.

Before you were born, God saw your substance and the structure of your life. He saw you as a water-walker, someone willing to venture out on the instability of turmoil to face the storm and conquer its brute force. He saw you as someone willing to put the devil under your feet and keep pressing toward destiny.

> *Fear not, for I have redeemed you; I have called you by your name; You are Mine. When you pass through the waters, I will be with you; and through the rivers, they shall not over-flow you. When you walk through the fire, you shall not be burned, nor shall the flame scorch you. For I am the* LORD *your God.* (Isaiah 43:1–3)

Whether you're walking on the instability of water in the midst of a storm, or whether you've been thrown in the fire, do not be afraid, but lean on the Lord and His promises. Then, whatever you walk upon will be yours!

CHAPTER THREE

WHATEVER WAS…IS!

WHATEVER WAS...IS!

I have seen the God-given task with which
the sons of men are to be occupied.
He has made everything beautiful in its time.
Also He has put eternity in their hearts.
—Ecclesiastes 3:10–11

Romans 8:29–30 says,

For whom He foreknew, He also predestined to be conformed to the image of His Son, that He might be the firstborn among many brethren. Moreover whom He predestined, these He also called; whom He called, these He also justified; and whom He justified, these He also glorified.

The exciting part about this passage is that it is expressed in the past tense. These things have already been accomplished. You are called, justified, and glorified, and you are currently in the process of becoming who you already are—the person

God designed. God designed you knowing your purpose and destiny. In the heavenly realm, He made provision for all your needs before they ever appeared.

In Luke, the Pharisees demanded to know when the kingdom of God would come. Jesus simply answered,

> *The kingdom of God does not come with observation; nor will they say, "See here!" or "See there!" For indeed, the kingdom of God is within you.* (Like 17:20–21)

Everything you need to accomplish your purpose and fulfill your destiny is in the kingdom, and the kingdom lies within you. That's why 1 John 4:4 says, *"You are of God, little children, and have overcome them, because He who is in you is greater than he who is in the world."* The Creator of all things, the Author and Finisher of all things, resides within you, and in Him is your every answer. Take a look at Ecclesiastes 1:9, *"That which has been is what will be, that which is done is what will be done, and there is nothing new under the sun."* Nothing that we do, see, or experience is new. There is nothing new under the sun.

YOU ARE CURRENTLY IN THE PROCESS OF BECOMING WHO YOU ALREADY ARE—THE PERSON GOD DESIGNED.

STEP INTO THE ETERNAL

Most of us have heard many wonderful messages on "the great exchange"—messages concerning the substitutionary work of the Lord Jesus Christ. These are messages that we need to hear often. For instance, Jesus died so that we might live. He bore our sicknesses so that we might walk in health. He became poor so that we might be rich. He became sin so that we might be righteous. This is the greatest story ever told—the great exchange.

But there is a very pertinent fact that we often leave out of this wondrous work. Without this important awareness, we will find it extremely difficult to enter the land of promise that God has prepared for us before the foundation of the world. Too often we neglect the importance that Jesus stepped out of eternity and into time, so that you and I might have the ability to step out of time and into eternity. For far too long we've been limited to Adam's clock, living out our lives stagnated by physical space and time. Jesus became the bridge to the timeless, and because of that, we can cross the same bridge, rejecting the confinements of time while embracing the promises of eternity.

JESUS STEPPED OUT OF ETERNITY AND INTO TIME, SO THAT WE MIGHT HAVE THE ABILITY TO STEP OUT OF TIME AND INTO ETERNITY.

The question then becomes, "How do we step out of time and into the eternal and timeless?" You do it with your perception of the mighty name of Jesus, and you do it by faith. First John 5:4 says, *"For whatever is born of God overcomes the world. And this is the victory that has overcome the world; our faith."* It is our faith in God that overcomes the world. It is our faith in His faithfulness, and in His Word, that overcomes the world and defies the world system.

If you will, by faith, learn to perceive the future in the present, you will begin to enter into your land of promise. If you continue to view the past in the present, you will simply remain where you are. It's so important to realize that we must make this shift. We have to shift from "foundational faith" to "accomplishing faith."

What Have You Been Delivered To?

Most of those who come into the kingdom of God develop a foundational faith against what they have been delivered *from*. They know that they've been delivered from hell and eternal death, from the curse of the law, and from various addictions. They know that they've been delivered from oppressive spirits of the devil. They have no problem with their faith for such issues. But now, if you're going to press ahead toward the destiny to which you are called, you're going to need accomplishing faith, which reveals that *to* which you've been delivered.

When the Israelites were delivered from the bondage of Egypt, they knew that they'd been delivered by the hand of God. They left Pharaoh, his taskmasters, and all the bondage and cruelty behind them. Then, when they reached the Red Sea, they knew they were delivered from Pharaoh for sure, because the mighty breath of God parted the waters and then used them to destroy their enemy once and for all.

They knew very well what they had been delivered from, but it took them forty years to complete a journey that should have taken several days because they couldn't perceive what they had been delivered to. They kept viewing the past in the present. All they could see was what was behind them. They were bound by a slave mentality resulting from over four hundred years of oppression. This, in turn, eroded their faith as they grew selfish, self-reliant, and disobedient. Because of their disobedience, they wandered in circles for the next forty years, looking for something that was already there—because whatever was...is!

Like the Israelites, many of us wander about, desperately looking for what has always been there. We grow just as selfish and disobedient. We try to manipulate our own circumstances instead of trusting in God. We're so busy trying to create our "preferred" reality that our God-designed destiny passes us by. God wants you to shift from foundational-faith (viewing at the past in the present) into accomplishing-faith (viewing the future in the present), where you not only realize what you've been delivered from, but what you've been delivered to.

SITTING IN HEAVENLY PLACES

Receive that which is yours, and your every need will be supplied. The clothes that the children of Israel wore did not wear out in forty years. Their shoes didn't wear out, and they never missed a meal. If they ran out of water, God would bring forth water from a rock. The Lord says that the time for "manna mentality," living from miracle to miracle, is over. He now wants you to step over the Jordan and take what has already been prepared for you.

SITTING WITH JESUS IN HEAVENLY PLACES, YOU CAN SEE THINGS THE WAY GOD SEES THEM.

Everything you need to succeed already exists, but you must enforce and maintain what the Savior did in His death, burial, resurrection, ascension, and in His sitting at the right hand of the Father. I added the significance of seating, because He has also *"made us sit together in the heavenly places"* (Ephesians 2:6). It is in that place that you have the perfect vantage point to perceive your future in the present. It is there, sitting with Jesus in heavenly places, that you can see things the way God sees them.

SUCCESS IS NOT LOGICAL

In persevering, we often feel as if we've reached our maximum potential, which is a good thing, because that's exactly where God wants you to be. At your maximum capacity, you've entered the space where only God can do the rest and finish the course. In your weakness, His strength becomes evident. In your lack of knowledge, His understanding takes over and propels you beyond your natural capabilities.

Success is not logical. We have been trained by a society that strives to be logical, but the Lord asks us to rely on His economy, realizing that His economy and His way of doing things is not logical. When you can't pay all the bills, it's only logical to hold on to your tithe (your weekly giving) and make it up later. But God says to pay your tithe, and if you keep His house full, He'll keep your house in abundance. He commands us not to rob Him in tithes and offerings. (See Malachai 3:8.)

Grace and forgiveness reign in the kingdom of God, but if you persist on reliving the past in the present and expecting a different result, you're operating in insanity. You can't keep doing the same things you've always done if you want things to change in the present and future. You must go to God and ask Him what you need to do differently in order to make the shift from foundational-faith to accomplishing-faith. You must make the shift to faith-awareness in order to sail through the journey and look at adversity as an opportunity to glorify God.

When you see the flames, you can't always run the other way. It's our natural instinct to run from fire, but God is saying to us, in effect, "In this spiritual battle, you must stand up to adversity and face the torrid flames of Satan's threats." In the name of Jesus, declare and decree your victory over every attack. Nothing is impossible to someone who truly believes the Word of the Lord.

> YOU MUST MAKE THE SHIFT TO FAITH-AWARENESS IN ORDER TO SAIL THROUGH THE JOURNEY AND LOOK AT ADVERSITY AS AN OPPORTUNITY TO GLORIFY GOD.

THE NEED HAS ALREADY BEEN MET

Peace and consolation is the knowledge that God has already provided for every need that will arise. Having faith in that promise will lead you into the land of promise. Your victory will come when you fully embrace it with your heart—by faith, not by the law. Moses died, but Joshua led the children of Israel into the land of promise through the designated route. To finally arrive at their preordained destination, the children of Israel had to carefully follow the Lord's commands. At the battle of Jericho, Joshua gave them God's orders: *"You shall not shout or make any noise with your voice, nor shall a word proceed out of your mouth, until the day I say to you, 'Shout!' Then you shall shout"* (Joshua 6:10). When they finally shouted, the walls came tumbling down. (See verse 20.)

As the Lord is leading you to victory, you must learn when to speak and when to keep silent. Like Israel, your very existence is often dependent upon how well you're able to hear and obey the voice of the Lord. *"To everything there is a season, a time for every purpose under heaven... a time to keep silence, and a time to speak"* (Ecclesiastes 3:1, 7).

NO MATTER WHAT HAS GONE ON IN YOUR PAST, GOD REMAINS COMMITTED TO YOUR PRESENT AND FUTURE.

The Israelites were commanded to supernaturally take that which God had already promised they would receive. (See Exodus 3:8.) In spite of their disobedience, the children of Israel eventually walked into the land of promise. The door that God opens, no man can shut. When He makes you a promise, no matter how long it takes, He makes good on His word.

No matter what has gone on in your past, God remains committed to your present and future. Past failures or successes are not going to give you what you need to enter your land of promise. There's only one way in and that is by faith in the purpose that God has designed on your behalf.

You accomplish this by perceiving the plans and purposes that God has designed and provided for your life. This is the kind of consciousness that must be adopted by the body of Christ. You must stop peering through the rearview mirror that hinders you from moving forward. You can go nowhere when all you do is look backward. You have to invoke your spiritual vision to actually look toward your destiny and begin to move forward in order to reach it.

SPIRITUAL ARMAMENT

The devil is crafty. Even so, we are creatures who have been given head-to-toe armor to defeat every foe. However, forward motion is required for this armament to be applied in battle. You can't turn around and run away, because you have a destination that must be reached. Know that you have authority over the devices of the enemy. As we read before, God says, *"Behold, I give you the authority to trample on serpents and scorpions, and over all the power of the enemy, and nothing shall by any means hurt you"* (Luke 10:19).

Know that when the threat is made, a defense has already been provided to combat it. The minute you start to think that there is no way of escape, God steps in and receives your burdensome load. As long as you walk according to His direction, you're going to conquer each new challenge in His strength and according to His power.

Second Corinthians 5:7 reminds us, *"For we walk by faith, not by sight."* That does not mean that we discount what we see. It means that we apply what God says in the spirit to our natural sight. We need to *"walk by faith, not by sight"* in all matters, knowing that God is with us and has promised us, *"I will never leave you nor forsake you"* (Hebrews 13:5).

No one can fathom the entirety of the work that God does from beginning to end:

> *I have seen the God-given task with which the sons of men are to be occupied. He has made everything beautiful in its time. Also He has put eternity in their hearts.*
>
> (Ecclesiastes 3:10–11)

When God plants eternity in your heart that means that you have, in your heart, a memory of God's design for your life.

When Elijah was told to go to the widow woman at Zarephath, God let him know that He'd already commanded the widow woman to sustain him. When he got there, she was already gathering sticks, preparing to cook her last meal. He approached her and asked for water, to which she agreed. *"As she was going to get it, he called to her and said, 'Please bring me a morsel of bread in your hand'"* (1 Kings 17:11). She quickly responded, *"I do not have bread"* (verse 12).

The widow consciously had no idea that a part of her destiny was to sustain this prophet of the Almighty. As recorded in Scripture, she replied,

> *As the LORD your God lives, I do not have bread, only a handful of flour in a bin, and a little oil in a jar; and see, I am gathering a couple of sticks that I may go in and prepare it for myself and my son, that we may eat it, and die.*
>
> (verse 12)

But Elijah assured her, in effect, "Just do what I tell you first, and you will be fine." Famine and drought had devastated the land. Yet, even with her son depending on her, this woman obeyed the word of the prophet. Why? In her heart she had a faint memory of her future destiny—a destiny that was unfolding that very day. In her heart she recognized the face that God had called her to sustain the man of God who stood before her.

Scripture tells us that eternity has been placed in our hearts, even if we don't consciously understand it. Let's look again at that passage from Ecclesiastes:

> *He has made everything beautiful in its time. Also He has put eternity in their hearts, except that no one can find out the work that God does from beginning to end.*
>
> (Ecclesiastes 3:11)

You will not necessarily know in your conscious mind all the things that God has put into your heart. You just have to know that there are things that He has put there. You only need to develop an awareness and recognition of them as they come forth.

SEE THE LIGHT

In your heart you can carry a memory of your calling and of the plans and purposes God has designed for your life. In your heart you know things that you cannot logically explain, but don't let that scare you or set you back. Don't allow that to keep you in the wilderness looking for something that is already within you. Jesus said, *"If you can believe, all things are possible to him who believes"* (Mark 9:23). The God who performed the creative work that we behold each day is living inside of us.

Walk in faith knowing that the God who made you knows about every barrier you will encounter throughout your journey. Be confident in knowing that you're another step closer to your purpose and destiny. *"We know that all things work together for good to those who love God, to those who are the called according to His purpose"* (Romans 8:28). Based on God's Word and His sovereign wisdom, everything you need to fulfill His will and purpose for your life is already in you, because whatever was...is!

> THE GOD WHO PERFORMED THE CREATIVE WORK THAT WE BEHOLD EACH DAY IS LIVING INSIDE EACH OF US.

CHAPTER FOUR

START WITH THE HEART PART

START WITH THE HEART PART

For man looks at the outward appearance,
but the Lord looks at the heart.
—1 Samuel 16:7

I n Mark 10:27, Jesus declared, *"With men it is impossible, but not with God; for with God all things are possible."* All things are possible to those who believe with heart-faith. In fact, the Lord was speaking directly to you in Jeremiah 29:11 when He said, *"For I know the thoughts that I think toward you, says the Lord, thoughts of peace and not of evil, to give you a future and a hope."* Here, we see God addressing two specific areas concerning His thoughts toward you and His plan for your life:

- He has good thoughts about you. You are on His mind.

- The Lord has plans for your future. As you live out your life and walk with God, He will lead you in divine purpose and destiny.

Many people are desperate, discouraged, and depressed in life because they feel that they have no future. They are without hope. They've been fed a lie of the enemy that says, because of their culture, level of education, or background, they have no future. In the last chapter, we learned that when you belong to Christ, you are Abraham's seed and an heir according to the promise. You have a future that will lead you toward your land of promise. You are not on this journey alone, for if you acknowledge the Lord in all of your ways, He will direct your path. (See Proverbs 3:6.)

My son, give attention to my words; incline your ear to my sayings. Do not let them depart from your eyes; keep them in the midst of your heart; for they are life to those who find them, and health to all their flesh. Keep your heart with all diligence, for out of it spring the issues of life.

(Proverbs 4:20–23)

You are here on purpose, and if you're going to live out your designed destiny, you're going to have to start with the "heart part" because out of the heart spring the issues of life. The Lord always starts with the heart part.

WHO'S THE PARTY FOR?

First Samuel gives an eye-opening account of how the Lord removed His anointing from King Saul because of his rebellion and disobedience. He spoke to the prophet Samuel and said, *"I am sending you to Jesse the Bethlehemite. For I have provided Myself a king among his sons"* (1 Samuel 16:1). Immediately, Samuel paused and said to the Lord, *"How can I go?*

If Saul hears it, he will kill me" (verse 2). The Lord comforted Samuel, *"Take a heifer with you, and say, 'I have come to sacrifice to the LORD.' Then invite Jesse to the sacrifice, and I will show you what you shall do; you shall anoint for Me the one I name to you"* (verses 2–3). So, Samuel obeyed the Lord and went to the house of Jesse in order to recognize the new king.

After he arrived, he made his sacrifices and paid homage unto the Lord and invited Jesse and his sons to his sacrifice. First, Jesse brought out his most eligible son, Eliab. Scripture says that he was tall and handsome, probably well accomplished in all aspects of life. Even Samuel, when he saw Eliab, agreed, *"Surely the Lord's anointed is before Him"* (1 Samuel 16:6).

But the Lord immediately warned Samuel,

Do not look at his appearance or at the height of his stature, because I have refused him. For the Lord does not see as man sees; for man looks at the outward appearance, but the LORD looks at the heart. (1 Samuel 16:7)

In other words, God starts with the heart part.

One after another, Jesse presented his sons. It's easy to imagine them, flexing their muscles and showing off their carved physiques, but Samuel refused every one of them. Seven sons were brought before Samuel, and seven sons were refused. Finally, Samuel inquired of Jesse, *"Are all the young men here?"* (verse 11). To which Jesse admitted, *"There remains yet the youngest, and there he is, keeping the sheep"* (verse 11). Jesse had not even thought of including this son. They didn't expect much from him. There was no hope or anticipation for his future design. In fact, he was kind of eccentric, playing his harp for the sheep and the stars.

But Samuel was not deterred. Instead he said, *"Send and bring him. For we will not sit down till he comes here"* (1 Samuel 16:11). This is when all of the brothers who'd been invited to the party finally sent for the one for whom the party had been planned in the first place.

When they found little David in the field, I imagine that he was singing or dancing, throwing rocks, or doing something to occupy his sheep-tending time. But when they brought David into the presence of God and the prophet laid his eyes on him, God declared, *"Arise, anoint him; for this is the one!"* (verse 12). The Lord had found *"a man after His own heart"* (1 Samuel 13:14, Acts 13:22). Samuel poured the horn of oil over David. When the oil came on David, the anointing remained on him for the rest of his life. Start with the heart, for out of the heart spring the issues of life. (See Proverbs 4:23.)

Heart Revelation

Look again at Mark 11:23, where Jesus said,

For assuredly, I say to you, whoever says to this mountain, "Be removed and be cast into the sea," and does not doubt in his heart, but believes that those things he says will be done, he will have whatever he says.

Those words, spoken by Jesus Himself, tell us that heart-faith can move a mountain and cast it into the sea. Romans 10:9–10 says,

If you confess with your mouth the Lord Jesus and believe in your heart that God has raised Him from the dead, you will be saved. For with the heart one believes unto righteousness, and with the mouth confession is made unto salvation.

The same principle applies throughout the Word of God. You will find that *"out of the abundance of the heart his mouth speaks"* (Luke 6:45). The body of Christ has been taught much about speaking, and we need to heed that teaching. However, we need to realize that if we're just speaking like parrots, and not speaking from the heart, the mountain won't move. But when your mouth speaks in conjunction with your heart, then that mountain has to move!

REVELATION DESTROYS THE WORKS OF EVIL AND ALL THAT THE ENEMY HAS SET AGAINST YOU.

Earlier I stated that the body of Christ often tries to proclaim the message of faith by ritual and formalism, but results are only experienced by first receiving revelation—heart-revelation. Revelation destroys the works of evil and all that the enemy has set against you. Merely copying what others have done will not work on your behalf. The only one you can copy successfully is Jesus Christ. You must have your own heart-revelation. You have to believe that He can do *"exceedingly abundantly above all that we ask or think, according to the power that works in us"* (Ephesians 3:20).

For too long we've been programmed to think that just because we practice a particular method, or have followed certain steps, that the mountain should move. In truth, the mountain doesn't move because you have to start with the heart part. The heart part is in knowing who you are, in whom you believe, and that God will never leave or forsake you. God is not a man that He should lie. (See Numbers 23:19.) If He said it, He'll do it; if He spoke it, He'll bring it to pass. If you're going to accomplish your purpose and fulfill your God-designed destiny, you need to start with the heart part.

Hundreds of people go to the altar to confess that Jesus Christ is Lord merely because someone instructed them to do it. They weren't speaking a confession of faith from the heart but were only following instructions. When they return to their seats, if they didn't truly believe what they're saying, I'm afraid they are no more saved than they were before they arose from their pew. Salvation is not about walking an aisle or saying the magic words—it's about the heart. That's not my opinion; that's according to Scripture:

> *If you confess with your mouth the Lord Jesus and believe in your heart that God has raised Him from the dead, you will be saved.* (Romans 10:9)

It only takes the twinkling of an eye, a microsecond, to be born again—a new creation. *"Therefore, if anyone is in Christ, he is a new creation; old things have passed away; behold, all things have become new"* (2 Corinthians 5:17). But it must happen in the heart. You must embrace your future and perceive it with your heart. If you only embrace it in your mind, it won't change a thing. You have to know in your heart that something great is ahead of you, that God has planned something for you that you can't imagine for yourself. You must speak from the heart or it is just talk with no evidence of change.

FUTURE MEMORY

You are on a path headed toward purpose and destiny, but your journey will be greatly enhanced if you would begin to realize that your heart already knows the path of walking with God. Perhaps you're thinking to yourself, *But my heart doesn't know.* You may not consciously know it, but God has placed eternity in your heart. All you have to do is seek Him for revelation on where He is trying to lead you.

God wants us to dig up the rich nuggets that He has placed deep within His Word. It's time to stop being dissuaded by the adversity of the devil—every trick, lie, and scheme that he sets against us. Beginning now, we need to put his every attack under our feet according to God's power. According to His dominion and glory, it's time for us to stop feeling threatened, and instead look at adversity as an opportunity to glorify the Lord. When you start with the heart part, all things become possible.

THE INNER MAN

In Romans 12:1, we are told to *"present [our] bodies a living sacrifice, holy, acceptable to God, which is your reasonable service." "Your reasonable service"* means that it is the least you can do; after all, if Jesus died for you, then you ought to be willing to live for Him. However, you can't present your body as a living sacrifice unless you start with the inner man, the heart part.

The decisions you make in life ultimately affect your inner being, the heart. Chapter four of Proverbs provides some very specific instructions in preserving the purity of the heart:

77

Keep your heart with all diligence, for out of it spring the issues of life. Put away from you a deceitful mouth, and put perverse lips far from you. Let your eyes look straight ahead, and your eyelids look right before you. Ponder the path of your feet, and let all your ways be established. Do not turn to the right or the left; remove your foot from evil.

(Proverbs 4:23–27)

This Scripture stresses the importance of protecting the inner man (the heart) by disciplining the outer man.

At women's conferences at our church, my wife Yolanda always gives a brief exhortation before introducing the speaker. She jokingly calls this her "little ditty," but what she calls her "little ditty" is usually a giant nugget!

THE DECISIONS YOU MAKE IN LIFE ULTIMATELY AFFECT YOUR INNER BEING, THE HEART.

In one particular instance, she read Proverbs 4:23, emphasizing that within the heart lie the issues of life. She then pointed out that we must not interpret the issues of life to mean only those that are positive, but also those that are negative. Therefore, we must guard our hearts diligently, because the heart is the master control of life. A wrong heart produces a wrong life. Whatever the heart loves, the ears will hear and the eyes will see.

Be cautious of what you say.

Put away from you a deceitful mouth, and put perverse lips far from you. (verse 24)

Be cautious of what you see.

Let your eyes look straight ahead, and your eyelids look right before you. (verse 25)

Be cautious of where you go.

Ponder the path of your feet, and let all your ways be established. Do not turn to the right or the left; remove your foot from evil. (verse 25–26)

The mouth and the heart are in close alignment. Jesus said, *"Out of the abundance of the heart the mouth speaks"* (Matthew 12:34). How can you possibly begin to align your mouth with God's Word unless you start with the heart? *"Death and life are in the power of the tongue"* (Proverbs 18:21). The perversity of the lips cannot be prevented unless you start with the heart and present your body as a living sacrifice.

> THE PERVERSITY OF THE LIPS CANNOT BE PREVENTED UNLESS YOU START WITH THE HEART.

Your mouth must be obedient to your heart where you consciously decide that your lips will not articulate anything that is not in the heart. When your mouth stops spewing wrong things or speaking contrary to the Word of God, then your eyes can become focused on Jesus, who is the Author and Finisher. *"He who has begun a good work in you will complete it until the day of Jesus Christ"* (Philippians 1:6). He who begins it will complete it.

When you start with the heart part, not only will you speak according to God's Word and keep your eyes focused upon Him, but your feet will stay on the narrow path. But you must start with the very core of your existence. You must begin by searching the heart to remove those things that are not like God.

King David was anointed king as a boy, and God called him *"a man after My own heart"* (1 Samuel 13:14, Acts 13:22). Along his journey, David was not immune to acting foolishly and even sinfully, but when he failed he went before God pleading, *"Create in me a clean heart, O God, and renew a steadfast spirit within me. Do not cast me away from Your presence, and do not take Your Holy Spirit from me"* (Psalm 51:10–11). David was far from perfect, but he was a man who had a heart for God, and God had a heart for him.

A PERFECTED HEART

Do not turn to the right or the left; remove your foot from evil. (Proverbs 4:27)

Every place that the sole of your foot will tread upon I have given you. (Joshua 1:3)

So much of our concern these days is in how we appear before others, instead of being concerned about whether we appear holy and acceptable before God Himself. We can do things in front of others to make them think that we're doing well because they can't see the innermost parts of our hearts. We can fool our brothers and sisters, and we can appear as if we are *holier-than-thou*, that our ducks are arranged neatly in a row. But God sees our hearts.

Our primary concern should be, "What does God see?"

Don't worry about what your pastor, your friends, or your family sees—worry about what God sees. Concern yourself

80

with great vigor how you appear before the Lord because He's the one who truly matters. And while we do need to be confident that our brothers and sisters love us, and that we give love to them as well, that should not be our primary focus. The focus is in allowing God to continually be perfecting the heart within you. You will always have some areas to work on and discipline, but when God sees a continually perfected heart, He will deliver you out of

> WE CAN FOOL OUR BROTHERS AND SISTERS, BUT GOD SEES THE HEART.

seemingly impossible situations, forgive you, and even make you look good when you don't deserve it. *"For His mercy endures forever"* (Psalm 136:1).

Second Corinthians 5:21 says, *"For He* [God] *made Him* [Jesus] *who knew no sin to be sin for us, that we might become the righteousness of God in Him."* In other words, Jesus, who never committed any sin, voluntarily took upon Himself the sins of the world. He nailed all of our sins to the cross, blotting them out on our behalf once and for all. And because of that, when you call upon His name in faith, He makes an exchange with you—giving you His righteousness and taking away your filthy rags.

Positionally, you are the righteousness of God. God the Father sees you through the filter of the blood of His Son. He sees you as pure, as righteous. That is why 2 Corinthians 5:17 says, *"If anyone is in Christ, he is a new creation; old things have passed away; behold, all things have become new."* If you're in Christ, you're a new creation. The old things are a part of your past. Your new life is a mind-set, which is continually being developed and renewed into the mind of Christ.

Remember that *old-things-passing-away* is a process, and it is out of that process that all things are becoming new. Nevertheless, positionally you are already a finished work as far as God is concerned. Right now you are in the process of becoming who He has designed you to be, but you must start with the heart if you're going to finish your course.

RELOCATE YOUR HEART

"A wise man's heart is at his right hand, but a fool's heart at his left" (Ecclesiastes 10:2). This is a rather confusing passage of Scripture. Since a person's heart is always found anatomically just to the left side of the human chest, what could this be referring to? It is my belief that Solomon, the author, as well as God Himself, was writing about the spiritual location of a person's heart. In biblical symbolism, the left side is the state of the natural man— fallen, limited, and even foolish. The right side is the spiritual side—God's blessings are often portrayed in Scripture as from God's right hand, Jesus is said to be sitting at God's right hand. Even though, physically, your heart remains on the left side of your chest, this Scripture is saying that you need to supernaturally move it to the right side or, in other words, begin operating with the heart and

REMEMBER THAT *OLD-THINGS-PASSING-AWAY* IS A PROCESS, AND IT IS OUT OF THAT PROCESS THAT ALL THINGS ARE BECOMING NEW.

mind of Christ. Otherwise, you will continually act out the foolishness of man-made thinking.

Our daily responsibility is to renew our minds and present our bodies as a living sacrifice, never conforming to this world, but transforming our minds with the Word of God to prove the good, acceptable, and perfect will of God. (See Romans 12:1–2.) By applying the Word, you are moving your heart to the right position. Although physically it remains in the same position, in the spiritual realm your heart has been repositioned to receive the wisdom of God. Your actions and thought will be spiritual instead of natural, wise instead of foolish.

What is your stand regarding sin? Do you rebuke every manner of sin in your life? Is your heart on the right side when it comes to anything that is evil? If you find yourself tolerating your old sinful nature, then your heart is shifting back into its natural position. It is your duty to supernaturally move it to the right hand where it will function for the glory of God.

The most effective way to move your heart to resist sin is through prayer and much fasting. When the topic of fasting surfaces, people often shy away and conclude that it is a thing of the past and an unnecessary part of the Christian walk. Unfortunately, this erroneous way of thinking has deprived many men and women of God of complete spiritual fulfillment, great spiritual power, and intimacy with God the Father. God is looking for people who dare to live a fasted life. Fasting is not merely a matter of skipping meals. A fasted life is being fully reliant on God and disciplined in how you live—that everything you do might glorify God.

Many wonderful men and women of God who rarely go on a food fast still live a fasted life. They simply avoid doing things that will not glorify the Lord. They are disciplined. They know, according to the spiritual location of their heart, the areas in which they need to be disciplined, and they act accordingly. If you know you have problems in certain areas, then you have to keep your heart firm and planted on the right side in those areas.

"That is why, for Christ's sake, I delight in weaknesses, in insults, in hardships, in persecutions, in difficulties. For when I am weak, then I am strong" (2 Corinthians 12:10 NIV). Every weakness in your life should become a strength because you've shifted over supernaturally. Now, when you are weak, He's strong. You become the supernatural individual that God has called you to be.

In Philippians 4:13, God has planted a gentle reminder on your behalf: *"I can do all things through Christ who strengthens me."* Nothing is impossible for you through Christ. In your own strength you will encounter innumerable impossibilities, but not with God. With God, the One who strengthens you, all things are possible.

Spiritually Ambidextrous

In 1 Chronicles 12:1–2, David was on the run, a fugitive from his father-in-law, Saul, who didn't want him to become king.

Now these were the men who came to David at Ziklag while he was still a fugitive from Saul the son of Kish; and they were among the mighty men, helpers in the war, armed with bows, using both the right hand and the left in hurling stones and shooting arrows with the bow. They were of Benjamin, Saul's brethren.

Using both the right and the left hand, they hurled stones and shot arrows. When you relocate your heart, God wants you to put the left side—the natural man—under subjection. He wants your natural man to act by the command of the right hand. Spiritually speaking, he wants you to be both right- and left-handed as you are led by His Spirit.

These men wanted to serve their king so much that they perfected their left hand according to their right, or their right according to their left. Some people are right-handed while others are left-handed, but these men were equally skillful with both hands. God desires us to become spiritually ambidextrous. He wants us to become capable of handling everything spiritually, both hands operable, and both hands just as strong.

When the natural side is in obedience to the relocated heart, we begin to see the manifestation of all things working together for the good. Your weak areas become your strengths, and your strengths become subject to Christ, causing your life to become spiritually balanced. God wants you to give it your all for His glory, a warrior able to hurl the rock at evil and become the arrow of every prophetic word into the heart of every adversity with accuracy.

According to Ecclesiastes 10:2, if you're using the left side, you're foolish, but if you relocate your heart to the right side and conduct your life, both spiritually and naturally, according to the relocated heart, you empower yourself to walk into God's promise for your life. What others think of your outward works and ability is not of utmost importance. Your primary concern should be on what God is seeing and performing within you. Is your heart in the proper location? Is your heart walking in a power and authority that causes your mouth to obey God's will and His way? Are your eyes focused on the Author and Finisher of all things? Are your feet firmly planted on the rock because you've taken the initiative to start with the heart? God's mandate today is to start with the heart part. Everything else will follow.

CHAPTER FIVE

YOUR DESTINY IS YOUR BIRTHRIGHT

YOUR DESTINY IS YOUR BIRTHRIGHT

*I call heaven and earth as witnesses today against
you, that I have set before you life and death,
blessing and cursing; therefore choose life, that both
you and your descendants may live.*
—Deuteronomy 30:19

G od's thoughts concerning you are great because He
thinks about you according to His purpose for your
life, not according to what you have or have not
accomplished.

*For I know the thoughts that I think toward you, says the
LORD, thoughts of peace and not of evil.* (Jeremiah 29:11)

You are in the process of becoming what God has designed
you to be. Don't be swayed by what you see in the natural;
look only at what the Lord has written about you. He has good
thoughts, thoughts of peace and not of evil, that you might

89

experience and accomplish your expected end. As heirs to God's promise, your destiny is your birthright. It's the life you were born to accomplish.

> *Blessed is the man who trusts in the LORD, and whose hope is the LORD. For he shall be like a tree planted by the waters, which spreads out its roots by the river, and will not fear when heat comes; but its leaf will be green, and will not be anxious in the year of drought, nor will cease from yielding fruit.* (Jeremiah 17:7–8)

You were created to be a fruit-bearing tree. If you put your trust in the Lord, you will bear much fruit in *every* season. That means you are called to bear fruit in spite of your present circumstances. When the devil turns up the heat of adversity in your life, when you're cold and lonely, or even during seasons when it seems as if no one else cares, you are supposed to bear fruit. But you don't have to do it on your own strength. You are planted beside rivers of living water, a tree that yields its abundance in spite of inclement weather.

GROW TO YOUR FULL POTENTIAL

In the Gospels, Jesus often compared us to fruit-bearing trees:

> *Even so, every good tree bears good fruit, but a bad tree bears bad fruit.* (Matthew 7:17)

> *You did not choose Me, but I chose you and appointed you that you should go and bear fruit, and that your fruit should remain.* (John 15:16)

God doesn't want bad fruit; He wants fruit that will remain. And He has determined that you will be a fruit-bearing tree.

When you look at a tree, have you ever wondered, *How did the tree get that way? How tall can a tree grow? How does it withstand the severity of the weather?* A tree is designed to grow to its full potential. It almost never has any problems reaching that potential because a tree doesn't have an ego. Ego is who you think you are or who you think you should be. Therefore, because a tree is created by God and designed to grow to its full potential, it doesn't decide, "That's not for me." A tree doesn't contradict its destiny and purpose. It just grows to its full potential.

You are designed to achieve and grow to your full potential. You are not designed to fall behind. Failure is not in God's plan for your future.

YOU ARE DESIGNED TO ACHIEVE AND GROW TO YOUR FULL POTENTIAL. FAILURE IS NOT IN GOD'S PLAN FOR YOUR FUTURE.

In all things, He causes us to triumph. We are above and not beneath (see Deuteronomy 28:13), and we are more than conquerors through the blood of Jesus Christ. (See Romans 8:37.) We are called to be kings and priests unto the Father (see Revelation 1:6) through the blood of the Son. Those are words that speak directly to your potential and future success.

How hard does a tree work to grow like it does? How much conscious effort does a tree make in order to grow to its full potential? It makes absolutely no conscious effort at all—the tree simply grows. Don't allow yourself to become so consumed with how you're going to make things happen when God has already made things happen for you. Simply follow His instructions, in faith, knowing that God has prepared the way for you to follow.

LIVING WATER

Allow His Word to water your seed and He will bring the increase. He is the supernatural power of the universe that works in you to accomplish your purpose and fulfill your destiny. It's *"not by might nor by power, but by My Spirit"* (Zechariah 4:6) that you're able to grow and bear fruit. Never in your life have you walked by an apple tree and heard it straining to grow and produce fruit. It merely does that which it was created to do—produce apples.

The apple is the fruit of the tree, a realization of the tree's destiny. You are a living tree, planted by living water, called to bring forth much fruit. Your fruit will come forth without you trying to force it because God knows the time and the season for each tree to yield its glorious fruit. During the process of growth, there is adversity, but He made this promise: *"I am the vine, you are the branches. He who abides in Me, and I in him, bears much fruit; for without Me you can do nothing"* (John 15:5).

The trials and adversities that the devil tosses into your path are no match for the power of God. Remember that success is not a destination; it is a journey. If you travel that journey by faith and embrace the outcome of every step you take, then your journey will produce fruit and you will become that magnificent tree, planted by the rivers of living water, rooted and grounded to produce purpose.

Then, when the trials of life cause you to feel dry and unloved, God brings His water of life into your irrigation channels. He irrigates your heart and allows your roots to grow deep. The water that came forth from the pierced side of the Savior has already provided a river of life for your existence, along with the authority and right to obtain all that He has created you to achieve. Your destiny and success are your birthright as a child of God.

LIMITLESS SEED

Some people look around aimlessly for God to give them what they need when He has already provided a limitless amount of seed that will provide for everything they need according to His riches in glory. In the walk of faith, the provision for our every need is not always seen with the natural eye. But with every step you take, each need is met. That is the true walk of faith.

For too many children of God, there is absolutely too much effort going forth in the wrong areas of life. Your effort should be spent on believing the Word of God and standing on what God has designed on your behalf. Then you will be able to walk on the waters of this world. Every tree knows that it's a tree. It's planted, it grows, it fulfills its destiny, and it doesn't try to contradict or go against the design that God has for it.

God is hungry for those who will walk according to His Word. *"We should no longer be children, tossed to and fro and carried about with every wind of doctrine, by the trickery of men, in the cunning craftiness of deceitful plotting"* (Ephesians 4:14). He thirsts for people who will stand and not be swayed to the left

93

or to the right by every wind of doctrine or adversity. Your destiny and design is a part of your birthright. No man can take it from you and no devil can revoke it or steal its many benefits. You simply need to choose it for yourself.

Many times, we hinder our own growth by becoming victims of our conditioning—all the data that has been placed in us from the time we were born. When I look at a little baby who's smiling, I get an uncontrollable urge to smile too. Why? Because that baby stirs up something in my memory, a blissful era of happiness I enjoyed before the world contaminated me and overloaded me with all the data with which I now live. That baby reminds me that I have a memory in my heart of that smile that was so pure, so honest, and so carefree.

> WITHOUT FEAR THERE WOULD BE NO LIMITS TO WHAT YOU COULD DO.

There aren't many things that frighten a baby. They will cry because of some unmet need, but they do not scare easily. Perhaps it is because they are so completely dependent on everyone around them. Or, perhaps it is because their imaginations are not yet creating frightening possibilities. Can you imagine if you walked with that kind of childlike faith—a faith without fear? What could you accomplish if you could become the little child that Jesus welcomed to come unto him in order to experience the kingdom of God. Without fear there would be no limits to what you could do.

Babies are a clean slate. They haven't been marked up by the world. They haven't a care until that very same world that they are enjoying and experiencing begins to contaminate them by telling them what they can and cannot do. Eventually the world tells them that they are intelligent or ignorant, talented or untalented, too short for the job or perhaps too tall. Others will tell them that they come from the wrong side of the tracks or, the devil's favorite, that they are the wrong color. Little by little, the world contaminates that baby so that by the time he is five or six years old, he has already developed an ego—an expectation of how things should be within his environment—that might be contrary to God's design and destiny.

A CORPORATE MATTER

Ego is your worst enemy. It tells you that you should have a healing ministry when in reality you should be part of an intercessory ministry. Ego causes you to become disconnected and out of place. It causes you to look at yourself separately and individually rather than as a holistic element of the body. Scripture says that Jesus is the head and we, the church, are the body—members one of another. (See Colossians 1:18 and Romans 12:5.) Ego causes us to disregard the other members and, instead, adapt an elitist attitude of territorialism that says, "This is my ministry!" Ego ignores the proper guiding and instruction from the Lord that is needed to fulfill our call effectively.

In Joshua 1:2, when the Lord said to Joshua, *"Moses My servant is dead,"* He was announcing a new way of entering, receiving, and achieving. He made it known that His people would no longer be a one-man ministry. In effect, He was saying, "Joshua, it's your turn. Rise up and lead these people."

The victories that came forth as they entered the Promised Land were now more than one man doing miracles with his staff; now they were a corporate, or community, effort.

Ego causes separatism in the body of Christ and threatens to erode and destroy community. Rout out ego and watch the Lord begin to grow you to your full potential. Stop letting your ego tell your Creator and Designer what type of leaves should be on your tree and how far your branches should stretch out. Your ways are not God's ways; you cannot dictate how the branches of your purpose and destiny are to be placed. When you do, it is your ego that holds you back from fulfilling your true potential. A tree grows to its full capacity and fulfills its design. But if a tree is planted in the desert, it has a different design than one that is planted in the rich soil of the Sequoia National Forest. That's why it is important to know where you're planted. You are a tree planted by rivers of living water.

Success is not a pipedream; it is your birthright because God designed and called you to a purpose and also gave you the means to reach that end.

God is not a man, that He should lie, nor a son of man, that He should repent. Has He said, and will He not do? Or has He spoken, and will He not make it good?

(Numbers 23:19)

For all the promises of God in Him are Yes, and in Him Amen, to the glory of God through us.

(2 Corinthians 1:20)

Once you become aware of the fact that what belongs to you is yours, by God's power and grace, then His promises will become a living, active ingredient in your life.

STRIDE TOWARD DESTINY

You are like a fingerprint—one of a kind, intricately designed by God. In His perfect timing, your purpose shall be revealed as you walk with Him. God doesn't leave you or forsake you. He will stand with you through thick and thin. Even when you fail, He's the one who will pick you up. Even when you are knocked down, God will give you the ability to stand again. He's the one who walks right next to you, strengthens your foundation, and gives you the ability and courage to fulfill your destiny.

> IN GOD'S PERFECT TIMING, YOUR PURPOSE SHALL BE REVEALED AS YOU WALK WITH HIM.

Many good men and women are walking despite the fact that they have been knocked off their feet. How? Because even in their incapacitated state, they continue to follow God's diet to build strength and continue moving. Inner perseverance is a gift from God that keeps the believer on the path of righteousness despite the obstacles that he or she might face along the way.

> *And let us not grow weary while doing good, for in due season we shall reap if we do not lose heart.*   (Galatians 6:9)

God is calling people who are willing to stand on the promise and upon the rock of His Word. Your perception about yourself will create your reality. You already have ability and creativity; after all, God made you in His own image and likeness. It is His anointing and His glory that does the creating, but He chooses to use you to help bring it to pass.

The Gift of Choice

Your destiny is your birthright, but it is also a choice you must make and embrace.

You must perceive what has been written on your behalf and begin to apply it by faith. Jesus said, *"Heaven and earth will pass away, but My words will by no means pass away"* (Luke 21:33). God's Word is eternal. It always was, and it always will be. Isaiah 40:8 drives this point home, *"The grass withers, the flower fades, but the word of our God stands forever."*

God's Word is eternal and He doesn't want you making decisions based on the temporary, but according to His eternal wisdom. As you begin to see things in the light of God's Word, you will begin to see yourself written in His book and begin to realize that your destiny is truly your birthright. But it is a destiny that you can either reject or accept.

The ability to choose is what separates mankind from all other creatures. Every man and woman, always and without exception, has been given the gift of choice.

> *I call heaven and earth as witnesses today against you, that I have set before you life and death, blessing and cursing; therefore choose life, that both you and your descendants may live.* (Deuteronomy 30:19)

Unlike a tree that merely grows without the ability to choose how tall it's going to be or where it has been planted, God has given you a marvelous gift called *choice*—free will. God will not force His love, blessings, and plans upon His children.

Consequently, the ability to choose can sometimes be our greatest handicap. You have the option to either cooperate with God's purpose and destiny for your life or reject it. Whether or not you grow to your full potential will ultimately depend upon the choices you make. Choice always provides you with alternatives. The choice that many have erroneously made is choosing a negative alternative.

WHETHER OR NOT YOU GROW TO YOUR FULL POTENTIAL WILL ULTIMATELY DEPEND UPON THE CHOICES YOU MAKE.

The magnificence of God, however, is grace. He has said that anytime, anywhere, *"whoever calls on the name of the LORD shall be saved"* (Joel 2:32, Romans 10:13). If you're sinking while trying to walk on the water, all you have to say is, "Lord, save me." He will hear your cry, reach down, pick you up, and walk to the preordained destination with you. When God gives you the ability to choose, do you choose the purpose and destiny that He saw before He formed you, or do you choose according to your ego?

Because that, when they knew God, they glorified him not as God, neither were thankful; but became vain in their imaginations, and their foolish heart was darkened.

(Romans 1:21 KJV)

Ego causes you to turn your back on your God-given opportunity to experience greatness in Him, and instead settle for mediocrity in yourself. The days of wanting everything to go your way must fall by the wayside.

Casting down imaginations, and every high thing that exalteth itself against the knowledge of God, and bringing into captivity every thought to the obedience of Christ.

(2 Corinthians 5:10 KJV)

It is not just a suggestion. God is commanding you to cast down all vanity, all vain imaginations, and to join together with your brothers and sisters to build the kingdom of God. In doing so, God will supply your every resource and need according to His riches in glory, but you must make the choice.

RIGHTFUL POSITION

What feels good is not always the best option. The Holy Spirit must be your guide. He is the one who leads. *"For as many as are led by the Spirit of God, these are sons* [and daughters] *of God"* (Romans 8:14). Begin to live your life circumspectly according to God's intention for your life and nothing will be able to hold you back or hinder your destiny. It is your birthright. It's what you were called to do, and success is in your future. God did not design you for failure but gave you everything that you need to finish your course. But again, the choice is yours.

I remember my days as a traveling minister. It was really carefree work compared to being the full-time pastor of a church. When you're a traveling minister, you don't necessarily carry the spiritual burden of tending the flock. Instead, you're constantly ministering to a new flock each week. You go in, minister the Word, and you heal in the name of Jesus, leaving everything else for the pastor to fix. I enjoyed that work for quite a few years and loved what I was doing. I was well respected and really enjoyed ministering the Word of the Lord throughout the country. Then, the Lord told me, "I want you to pastor a church." Immediately my ego kicked in, "But I'm not a pastor. I know my call and what I'm supposed to be." I'd even raise my voice when someone suggested anything contrary to my egotistical mind-set.

It took me six months to realize that God was actually calling me to pastor a church, and the rest is history. I know now that I am in my rightful position. God has been moving me into a place of responsibility over many ministries and churches in order to establish His kingdom. I am now walking out God's purpose and living out my birthright. I am operating through the destiny and design that God created for me, not the one that I thought was best.

Initially, I didn't realize what God had called me to accomplish. Though He still calls me to travel and preach as I once did, my true calling is to pastor a flock and raise them up to build the kingdom of God. Today, the Lord is using me to minister to apostles, prophets, evangelists, pastors, and teachers. I'm raising the five-fold ministry (apostle, prophet, evangelist, pastor, and teacher) in the power of God. (See Ephesians 4:11.) I love it because it's my birthright, my destiny, and what I'm called to do according to what God had designed and written about me before I was even born.

CHAPTER SIX

WHAT YOU DO IN LIFE ECHOES IN ETERNITY

WHAT YOU DO IN LIFE ECHOES IN ETERNITY

The grass withers, the flower fades,
but the word of our God stands forever.
—Isaiah 40:8

C an you imagine having access to everything necessary to meet your physical needs, yet finding yourself
living beneath a bridge and begging for scraps of food
from passers-by? Though everything that you could ever want
or need is easily available and accessible, instead you reject it
and live as one having no hope—homeless, wandering about
with no family, no loved ones, and no inheritance to sustain
your identity.

As outlandish as this may seem, many within the family
of God live beneath their means on a daily basis. As children
of God, we have this promise: *"My God shall supply all your need*
according to His riches in glory by Christ Jesus" (Philippians 4:19).
You have access to anything and everything there is to meet

105

your need, and you have access to this promise regardless of your present worldly surroundings.

How often we allow ourselves to be defined by the world's confining standards of growth: the ups and downs of Wall Street, the economy, and the natural circumstances and emotional state of our immediate surroundings. You need to rid yourself of all the negative databases you've received in your memory banks—false information that has limited your potential based on your natural I.Q., background, and human abilities. They have dictated your capabilities by informing you what you can or can't do. Begin now to update those files based on the design God has for you and renew your way of thinking. Only then will you be in the process of becoming the person who God has designed you to be.

> GOD'S WORD IS ETERNAL AND CANNOT BE ALTERED BY PRESENT CIRCUMSTANCES.

DON'T GET STUCK

God's Word is eternal and cannot be altered by present circumstances. First John 5:4 reminds us, *"For whatever is born of God overcomes the world. And this is the victory that has overcome the world; our faith."* It is our faith in God, and in His Word, that enables us to be world-overcomers. *"So then faith comes by hearing, and hearing by the word of God"* (Romans 10:17). In order to operate in this world, you're going to have to go out of your way to hear the Word of God—but it doesn't end there:

But be doers of the word, and not hearers only, deceiving

yourselves....faith by itself, if it does not have works, is
dead. (James 1:22; 2:17)

You must hear the Word, agree with it, and apply it to your life by becoming a doer of the Word and not a hearer only. Many people flood the church on Sunday shouting, "Amen... hallelujah," but ultimately return home to life as usual. Nothing has changed.

Back in the days when we played vinyl LP records, if the record was scratched, it would get stuck in one place going over and over the same spot, ruining our favorite song. That's the way some of our lives are. We're stuck playing the same old portion of the same old song. Because of the scratches and wounds we've received along life's way, we have become stuck and are no longer able to yield the melodious sounds of God.

We need a release to be propelled into destiny. The decisions you make today will echo for eternity. One of the enemy's greatest deceptions is to stagnate your growth and impede your future.

CULTIVATE THE POTENTIAL

This God of yesterday, today, and tomorrow knows the beginning from the end and the end from the beginning. In sports, when a good coach recognizes a player with promise, he cultivates that potential in his heart. But God is so sovereign and so filled with infinite supernatural ability, He saw your abilities before He formed you. He's thinking about things that you're going to do but haven't even accomplished yet. You're in the process of becoming the person that He had on His mind before eternity. You're in the process of winning what He already enabled you to win, buying what He already enabled you to buy, and thereby fulfilling your destiny.

Destiny Not Found in Religion

Perhaps you've been inquiring of God, "What is my purpose? What is my destiny? Why am I here?" As I stated earlier, as you begin to offer up your body as a living sacrifice and allow self-will to die, eventually you will begin to see the earthly manifestation of your spiritual destiny.

But you will never receive the full manifestation of God's will for your life by trying to conform to religion rather than pursuing a relationship with the Father. Too much "religiosity" and tradition attached to your walk of faith can become a great hindrance to your spiritual development. Prayer and fasting are important devotional tools for the body of Christ, and we need to practice both without making them the goal of our journey. They are a means, but not an end. Putting your faith and trust in prayer and fasting won't help you to discover and fulfill your destiny. That only happens when you put your invest yourself fully into a relationship with your almighty Father, who is in heaven.

Too often, we look for shortcuts in our spiritual life by expecting a seminar or lecture to reveal knowledge concerning our destiny. Certainly, God can choose to use anything and anyone to speak to us, but we must know that our destiny ultimately can only be revealed by the voice and will of God. Within the Word of God lies a lifelong seminar that declares, decrees, and defines who you already are and who you are in the process of becoming.

The fact of the matter is, we don't know exactly how we're going to reach our destiny or accomplish our purpose, but we must trust in the Father and know that He reveals all things in time. God instructed Abraham to pack his things and say good-bye to all of his relatives and the comforts of social status. He ordered Abraham to leave and travel to a land that he knew nothing about. (See Genesis 12:1.)

Abraham received this word and remains living proof that what we do in life echoes in eternity. He would become a father of nations, but all he did was follow God's instructions. He packed his belongings and said good-bye to his relatives. He didn't even do that perfectly. He took Lot with him, causing him much heartache later. (See Genesis 14 and 19.) Nevertheless, he obeyed God and went forth to fulfill the destiny that God had designed for him.

Today, thanks to Scripture, we know that we are kings and priests (see Revelation 1:6), joint heirs with Christ (see Romans 8:17), and more than conquerors through the blood of Jesus Christ. (See Romans 8:37.) We know that God causes us to stand in the face of all adversity. Abraham did not have these Scriptures. He had no idea what lay ahead, but because he obeyed the voice of God, his life continues to echo throughout eternity.

GOD CAN USE ANYONE

Some believers have already made up their minds that God could never use them to accomplish His will. In their minds, they don't have the education, the skills, or the experience to be of any use to Him whatsoever. Don't fall for this trap. God is no respecter of persons. (See Acts 10:34 KJV.) He will use anything and anybody. The truth is: it's not about you; it's about Him.

The story of Balaam is a prime example. Balaam was a Gentile prophet, a famous soothsayer who would pronounce a curse for money. (See Numbers 22 and 23.) Mosaic Law strictly prohibited these practices, but then, Balaam wasn't a Jew—he was a Gentile. Balaam was a bit of a dichotomy. He was a "prophet for hire," speaking with the authority of God at times, and using the power of demonism at other times.

GOD WILL USE ANYTHING AND ANYBODY. IT'S NOT ABOUT YOU; IT'S ABOUT HIM.

Prior to entering the Promised Land, the nation of Israel camped on the steppes of Moab. They had just defeated three armies and taken their land. When Balak, the king of Moab, saw this, he panicked. Balak was an astute king, but was without the military muscle to defend his nation against the powerful army of Israel. Then he came up with the idea of putting a curse on the Jews. However, Balak did not call upon his own cult priests to perform the curse, but sent a delegation to the most famous soothsayer of his day, Balaam. After much argument, Balaam agreed to return with them to Moab for the purpose of pronouncing a demonic curse on Israel.

As he journeyed toward the Israelites, an angel of the Lord tried to stop him. However, the angel was not visible to Balaam, he was only seen by the donkey on which Balaam rode. As the donkey continually tried to avoid the sword-bearing angel,

Balaam grew more and more abusive toward the animal until God finally gave the animal a voice.

> *Then the LORD opened the mouth of the donkey, and she said to Balaam, "What have I done to you, that you have struck me these three times?"....Then the LORD opened Balaam's eyes, and he saw the Angel of the LORD standing in the way with His drawn sword in His hand; and he bowed his head and fell flat on his face. And the Angel of the LORD said to him, "Why have you struck your donkey these three times? Behold, I have come out to stand against you, because your way is perverse before Me. The donkey saw Me and turned aside from Me these three times. If she had not turned aside from Me, surely I would also have killed you by now, and let her live."* (Numbers 22:28, 31–33)

The angel sent Balaam back on his way but instructed him to speak only the words that the Lord gave him. This is the only example of a talking animal in Scripture, but it was all that the Lord had at His disposal. Now, if the Lord can use a donkey to speak His will, don't you think that He might be able to use you?

Several years before becoming a pastor, I served as an elder at my home church. As elder, one of my duties was to pray for people. One Sunday morning, a man came up and informed me that he had been in all three services that day and that several elders had already prayed for him. But he was insistent that the Lord wanted *me* to pray for him. I told him that my prayers weren't any better than theirs, but he wouldn't take no for an answer.

I asked him what the problem was, and he said that he had water in his lungs. I then began to pray, but somehow, in the middle of my eloquent prayer, I began to babble on about *typewriters* of all things. I panicked, totally embarrassed as there were many listening to me. As far as I was concerned, the anointing had just left the building as I desperately tried to bring the prayer back to the man's lungs. Finally, with a sigh of relief, I ended the prayer and opened my eyes. To my amazement, his face was covered with tears.

"What happened?" I asked.

He said, "You don't understand. A few days ago, all my word processors were stolen from my garage. The insurance company refused to pay for them, claiming I had the wrong kind of lock on the door. But God just told me, through your prayer, that they would pay for all of them!"

Two weeks later, there he was, standing in the congregation, waving the check with a big smile on his face. It was then that I got the revelation: if God can use Balaam's donkey, He can surely use me!

Where God guides, He provides. Where God guides, He resides. When you don't know exactly how you're going to get from the beginning to the end, rest assured that you are in a good place because as you continually hear the Word of the Lord and become a doer of what you've heard, God is faithful to reveal all things on your behalf.

OUR HEAVENLY BRIDEGROOM

In Matthew, a woman with an alabaster box anointed

Jesus with precious ointment for His burial. Jesus responded,

Assuredly, I say to you, wherever this gospel is preached in the whole world, what this woman has done will also be told as a memorial to her. (Matthew 26:13)

There are some who believe that the box was her hope chest. In previous generations, when a girl became old enough to marry she would purchase an box, albaster or perhaps teak or rosewood depending on her station in life. She would place precious perfume in the box and seal it. Then the young girl would hide it in a safe place until her bridegroom would come. When she found him and the bridegroom asked for her hand in marriage, she'd go to her secret place and retrieve the alabaster box with all the precious ointments and perfumes. She would break it at the bridegroom's feet. In so doing, she was declaring, "My quest for a bridegroom, my quest for a lover, is now over. I have found my bridegroom and through him I will have everything that I need."

The Lord is revealing the same to us today.

Faith is the substance of things hoped for, the evidence of things not seen. (Hebrews 11:1)

And my God shall supply all your need.
(Philippians 4:19)

Now to Him who is able to do exceedingly abundantly above all that we ask or think. (Ephesians 3:20)

If today you would choose to take your hope chest, come to the Bridegroom's feet and break it, you choice will echo throughout all eternity. He is the heavenly Bridegroom.

God may send you an earthly spouse who serves certain purposes, but your heavenly Bridegroom knows everything you need—and He will supply it. The Lord wants you to be a doer of the Word that He has placed in your heart. But you must begin to walk out your purpose and destiny and learn to embrace the outcome of every step you take along the way. Each step you take reduces the gap between you and destiny. God has a designed great purpose for everything and everyone under the sun.

> The Lord wants you to be a doer of the Word that He has placed in your heart.

Come Forth!

In John 11, Jesus was teaching His disciples at the Jordan River, the very place where His cousin, John the Baptist, had baptized Him three years prior. While there, sisters Mary and Martha sent him a message regarding their brother, Lazarus: *"Lord, behold, he whom You love is sick"* (John 11:3). Jesus replied, *"This sickness is not unto death, but for the glory of God"* (verse 4). Then He continued to teach them there for two more days. The disciples probably wondered why Jesus was in no hurry to heal His friend.

Finally, He instructed the disciples, *"Let us go to Judea again....Our friend Lazarus sleeps, but I go that I may wake him up"* (verses 7, 11). Since they had been threatened by stoning if they ever returned to that region, his disciples questioned the wisdom of this decision. Taking Jesus literally, they suggested,

"Lord, if he sleeps he will get well" (verse 12). Jesus shot back, *"Lazarus is dead. And I am glad for your sakes that I was not there, that you may believe. Nevertheless let us go to him"* (verses 14–15). Then Thomas, ever the optimist, cynically affirmed that they were destined for death as well, *"Let us also go, that we may die with Him"* (verse 16). Thank God for His patience and mercy.

Jesus and His disciples traveled on to Bethany, but by the time they arrived, Lazarus had already been dead in the tomb four days. At that point, of course, Jesus could have simply raised Lazarus with just one word. But Lazarus had a purpose, and what happened to him that day now echoes in eternity.

As Lazarus lay in the grave, Jesus said, *"Take away the stone"* (John 11:39). In the Spirit, Jesus went to where Lazarus lay. With His words, He commanded, *"Lazarus, come forth!"* (John 11:43). Out stumbled Lazarus from the tomb, bound with grave cloths. The first thing Jesus commanded to the men by the tomb was to unwrap his hands and feet. I suppose Jesus could have done this Himself, but everyone had a purpose in this miracle. Even Martha and Mary's purposes were fulfilled. They're the ones who provoked Jesus to reveal, *"I am the resurrection and the life. He who believes in Me, though he may die, he shall live"* (John 11:25).

SCRIPTURE WAS WRITTEN FOR YOU

Every account within the Word of God has been placed there from eternity. Everything has a purpose and a destiny. There was a word that came to me early in my ministry. God had just saved me, and as I read His Word I saw that Stephen, when he was being stoned, cried out to the Lord. He did not cry out for his life. He cried out to the Lord to forgive those who were stoning him. (See Acts 7.) As I read this, somehow, it broke my heart. My Master saw my heartbreak over Stephen's actions long before he was ever stoned. I thought, *Part of the reason that this account of Stephen's life was recorded was for me!* It had been written for the multitudes, of course, but it was something that broke my heart. It broke my heart because I wondered, *How can this man do this? They're stoning him.*

It was exactly what I had to see and needed desperately to see at the time. There was a purpose for all of this just as there is a purpose for all things concerning you today. You must now begin to accomplish your purpose and become a doer of the Word, knowing that what you do echoes throughout eternity.

OVERCOMING FAITH

You're never too young or too old in the Lord to have God's Spirit speak directly to the issues in your life. If you will take your alabaster box, break it at the Master's feet, and allow His will to be done, the Spirit of the Lord will enlighten your understanding and supply your need according to His riches in glory. (See Philippians 4:19.) Too often, people become distracted by all those things in their periphery. They have bills that are overwhelming, a business gone bad, or a marriage on the rocks. What they have to do in order to experience change is get their life off the rocks and on the Rock of God—His solid foundation that sustains the cumbersome weight of mankind's trials.

Regardless of your situation, God has an answer. Though it may look in the natural like your need will never be met, your faith in God is a constant reminder that *all* things are possible to those who believe. *"Faith is the substance of things hoped for, the evidence of things not seen"* (Hebrews 11:1).

If you're in a place where you can't even think about your purpose or destiny, don't give up, but endure for a season and you shall reap if you do not faint.

> *By faith Moses, when he was born, was hidden three months by his parents, because they saw he was a beautiful child; and they were not afraid of the king's command. By faith Moses, when he became of age, refused to be called the son of Pharaoh's daughter, choosing rather to suffer affliction with the people of God than to enjoy the passing pleasures of sin, esteeming the reproach of Christ greater riches than the treasures in Egypt; for he looked to the reward. By faith he forsook Egypt, not fearing the wrath of the king; for he endured **as seeing Him who is invisible.***
>
> (Hebrews 11:23–27, emphasis added)

By faith, Moses endured when he could have chosen to live the life of royalty. Rather than compromise his spiritual stand by enjoying the pleasures of sin for a season, Moses decided to focus on what would yield the best results for his eternal destination. He chose *"to suffer affliction with the people of God."*

NEVER...NEVER...NEVER

Perhaps you are currently in a place where you can't see the light at the end of the tunnel: you're having problems with your children, your marriage, or you've started something you can't finish and there is no clear way to victory in sight. Don't give in to the devil's defeat. Instead, endure *"as seeing Him who is invisible."* In *"Him who is invisible"* is a memory of the victories still to come and a destiny to be lived out. Even as Moses *"endured as seeing Him who is invisible,"* so should we today. Comfort and assurance will not come from what you see, but from endurance and faith.

We have all walked through the darkness and gone to bed wondering, *God, when are You going to deliver me out of this valley experience? How long must I endure and should I just give up?*

> COMFORT AND ASSURANCE WILL NOT COME FROM WHAT YOU SEE, BUT FROM ENDURANCE AND FAITH.

Whatever you do, never give up. When you give up, you develop an unhealthy attitude about yourself. When you give up, you miss out on blessings that God has designed for you since the foundation of the world. When you give up, you limit God's use of your life.

When you give up, you're making some important statements:

- that God's Word only works some of the time, not all the time;

- that greater is he that is in the world than He who is in you;

- that God's Word is not strong enough to deliver.

When you give up, you are limiting yourself to your own

puny, human power instead of God's almighty and supernatural strength.

Winston Churchill was not only the Prime Minister of Britain during World War II, but he was also a great orator and statesman. History regards Churchill as not only experienced and accomplished, but also as a man filled with great wisdom. Few remember that he graduated from a small, private all-boys' institution, Harrow School, in the bottom third of his class. As far as the human eye could see, it didn't appear that Winston had much going for him. He wasn't very popular in school, and no one predicted a promising end for him, but that didn't stop him from attending military college.

After college, Churchill entered into military service for Great Britain in India and Africa. Later, he was twice elected Prime Minister during one of the most difficult times in Great Britain's history. Then, Harrow School, his alma mater, asked him to speak to their young men and give them advice on how to succeed.

As the story goes, the schoolmaster called the boys together and announced, "Guess who is coming? Winston Churchill! I want everyone to get plenty of sleep; I want you to come dressed in your best and prepared to take copious notes because this is a man who will teach you how to succeed in life."

The day finally arrived and there was Winston Churchill, sitting on the platform of Harrow School. As they introduced him, Churchill rose from his seat. He was a chubby, short man—not very handsome or altogether distinguished. He straightened and buttoned his coat and went to the microphone. As he cleared his throat, all the boys were on the edge of their seat in anticipation of the great wisdom that was about to pour out of this great statesman—one who had become something out of nothing. As legend has it, Churchill looked out over his audience and said, "Never give up; never give up...never, never, never...never give up." Then he turned around and returned to his seat.

I believe that God, by His Spirit, is saying to you, "Never give up...never, never, never...never give up." Never give up, because what you do in life echoes throughout eternity.

CHAPTER SEVEN

GOD'S CONCEPT
OF TIME AND REALITY

GOD'S CONCEPT OF TIME AND REALITY

*"For My thoughts are not your thoughts, nor are
your ways My ways," says the Lord.*
—Isaiah 55:8

Have you ever persevered in the spirit, seeking God ever so diligently, almost rushing Him to meet your need or bring your desire to fruition? And then, just as you begin to grow complacent and accept your miserable circumstances, God suddenly brings your request to pass. He met your need at a time that was most critical to your situation. Consequently, you become so exhilarated and awed by God's goodness and faithfulness that you experienced a spiritual growth that allowed you to truly be able to receive the blessings of God in your life.

The verse above is so true: *"'For My thoughts are not your thoughts, nor are your ways My ways,' says the LORD."* God sends

His Word to fulfill a specific purpose in your life at a predetermined time. But His concept of time and reality are not always congruent with what we feel is best for our lives. Nonetheless, when God speaks a specific Word it will be accomplished, but according to His predetermined time of making it a reality in our lives:

> *So shall My word be that goes forth from My mouth; it shall not return to Me void, but it shall accomplish what I please, and it shall prosper in the thing for which I sent it.*
>
> (Isaiah 55:11)

God's concept of time and reality is far different from ours. *"With the Lord one day is as a thousand years, and a thousand years as one day"* (2 Peter 3:8). That is why we must be careful to renew our minds on a daily basis and make His thoughts our thoughts, so that our ways can become His ways. He is the God of eternity.

THOUGH MANY THINGS WITH MEN ARE IMPOSSIBLE, THE POSSIBILITIES OF GOD ARE LIMITLESS.

> *Your eyes saw my substance, being yet unformed. And in Your book they all were written, the days fashioned for me, when as yet there were none of them.*   (Psalm 139:16)

The purpose of your life is far greater than what you think it is. Some people think their expected end is to have a certain job or to marry a certain person, but God's purpose for you is far greater than that. In fact, if you knew the fullness of your expected end, you would probably declare it to be quite impossible. That's why Jesus said, *"If you can believe, all things are possible to him who believes"* (Mark 9:23). Though many things with men are impossible, the possibilities of God are limitless.

There is no question about what God can or cannot do. He can do all things perfectly. The question is: Can you believe? Not for some things, but for *all* things through Christ, who is your power, your strength, and your authority. Are you open to the purpose and destiny that He has designed for your life?

HIS THOUGHTS, HIS WAYS

In the beginning was the Word, and the Word was with God, and the Word was God....And the Word became flesh and dwelt among us, and we beheld His glory.
(John 1:1, 14)

Jesus is the living Word that was made flesh. God's Word is eternal; it never ceases.

Heaven and earth will pass away, but My words will by no means pass away. (Mark 13:31)

Forever, O LORD, Your word is settled in heaven. Your faithfulness endures to all generations. (Psalm 119:89–90)

God's Word is timeless; it fits perfectly into every age. You can count on His Word today and you can count on His Word five thousand years from today because *"Jesus Christ is the same yesterday, today, and forever"* (Hebrews 13:8).

In the early years of my ministry, having received many directives from the Lord, I endeavored to obey them all with childlike faith. Eventually, however, everything seemed to be going wrong, especially in the financial arena.

As I reasoned according to my way of thinking, it appeared that I had done something wrong or missed the voice of God at some point altogether. I then began to seek the Lord for His correction, an answer, anything—but to no avail. For seven days I cried out continuously, still no answer.

I was desperate as I fell asleep one night. A couple of hours later, I woke myself up quoting aloud Isaiah 55:8: "'*For My thoughts are not your thoughts, nor are your ways My ways,*' *says the* LORD."

I got up, picked up my Bible, and began reading, attempting to figure out what the Lord was trying to tell me. After quite awhile of hearing nothing, the Spirit of the Lord said, "This is not the way it ought to be." I then began to engage in one of my many debating sessions. I said, "What do You mean, Lord?" He told me that He didn't want me to remain in my current state. He wanted me to make His thoughts my thoughts, so that my ways would become His ways. He wanted me to understand that what I was experiencing was adversity, not failure. I was making a mountain out of a molehill!

When the Lord spoke through the prophet Isaiah, He was intimating that He didn't want us to stay the same. Instead, He wanted us to make His thoughts our thoughts, so that our ways would become His ways. As God's people, we need to learn to think differently and see things differently. What you see is not always what you get; it depends on how you look at it. We need to learn to think according to God's concept of time and reality, not according to the world's programming and conditioning that we have received all our lives. We must purposefully change our minds and begin to think as He thinks. By learning to see things as God sees them, our whole outlook on life will be transformed by the renewing of our minds.

In 2 Kings, Elisha and his servant were surrounded by the Syrians. He didn't pray to God for deliverance, for rescue, or to keep them from becoming prisoners of war. Instead, Elisha prayed for his servant, *"LORD, I pray, open his eyes that he may see"* (2 Kings 6:17). Immediately, the young man's eyes were opened and he saw a vast array of chariots and the mighty army of angels that God had prepared to defend them. Elisha simply asked the Lord to let his servant see according to God's reality rather than his own.

> BY LEARNING TO SEE THINGS AS GOD SEES THEM, OUR WHOLE OUTLOOK ON LIFE WILL BE TRANSFORMED BY THE RENEWING OF OUR MINDS.

You cannot get beyond your limited mind-set unless you change your way of thinking according to God's Word.

> *I beseech you therefore, brethren, by the mercies of God, that you present your bodies a living sacrifice, holy, acceptable to God, which is your reasonable service. And do not be conformed to this world, but be transformed by the renewing of your mind, that you may prove what is that good and acceptable and perfect will of God.*　　(Romans 12:1–2)

Do not be conformed to the thoughts of this world, but be transformed by the renewing of your mind. Expand your mind with the Word of God. Mankind's mind has been besieged and poisoned by society for centuries. Society tells us what is possible and what is impossible—what we can and cannot do. But now the Lord says, in effect, "Expand your consciousness with the Word of God, because a mind that has been expanded by the Word of God will never return to its original state."

The Moving Rock

The Word of God reminds you, *"I can do all things through Christ who strengthens me"* (Philippians 4:13). For instance, if someone asks you if a rock is moving, you're going to think that's a pretty dumb question because rocks are stationery. They don't go anywhere. In truth, however, the earth and everything on it is moving through space at great speed. Which means, in reality, the rock *is* moving, but in order for you to understand that, you must change your reality.

Jesus is your rock. He is the Rock of ages, the Rock of your salvation, and He is moving on your behalf right now whether you see Him moving or not. He is moving in your family, in your marriage, in your health, in your business, and in your finances. *"Whatever things you ask when you pray, believe that you receive them, and you will have them"* (Mark 11:24). Even when you can't immediately see the physical manifestation of your blessing, continue to pray, believing that you have received it because your need has already been met in the mind of God.

Each living creature has its own perception of reality, which is why renewing your mind is so vitally important. A snail, for instance, can only see one image every four seconds. That means that most of what you and I see and experience is unavailable to the snail. We say that the snail is slow and just creeps along, but in the snail's reality he is moving along at a normal pace. We are moving many times faster than the snail. On the other hand, a fly is able to see the black images between the frames of a movie because they experience reality much faster than we do. That's why it's hard to catch a fly with our hands. In this scenario, we're much like the snail.

When you renew your mind, you have to think differently. Your reality has to go by the wayside as you adopt and live within God's concept of time and reality. No longer should you walk in the things that you've been conditioned to walk in. You must reprogram the computer. Snails, flies, and humans have different standards of time and reality. But God wants you to experience the goodness of His Word and to begin to walk in His reality, for you are made in the image and likeness of God. (See Genesis 1:26–27.)

The very moment you were born onto the earth, people began telling you who you were and you believed them. Now, He wants you to put aside what you heard all your life and find out what He has said about you since eternity. Find out who He has destined you to be. *"Now faith is the substance of things hoped for, the evidence of things not seen"* (Hebrews 11:1). Just because we do not immediately see substance does not mean that it doesn't exist. The Lord saw your faith before you were formed and wrote the days of your life down in His book before you ever got here.

Because of the world's conditioning, we automatically create our own limitations based on our limited resources. We need to shake off that old way of thinking. With God's unlimited resources, *all* things are possible within His concept of time and reality. When Paul was shipwrecked on the island of Malta, he shook off limited thinking. As he stirred up the wood in the fire, a snake attached itself to his hand, and he literally shook the snake off. (See Acts 28:3–5.) Anytime you put wood into God's fire, snakes are going to come out and try to attach themselves to your flesh. Like Paul, you have to shake them off immediately.

Our reality often causes us to fear and is a constant reminder of limitations, weaknesses, and lack, but when you factor in God's concept of time and reality you're reminded that *all* things are possible. Time is removed from the equation. Whenever a sinner calls out to Him, in a twinkling of an eye He sees that person as a re-created human being. This is not a concept you can understand from a textbook or determine from the reasoning of man. It is a spiritual truth that you must understand with your innermost being. You must embrace it and take it with you everywhere you go. Know that *"He who is in you is greater than he who is in the world"* (1 John 4:4).

A SEAT IN ETERNITY

God abides in eternity. He sees the present, past, and future simultaneously. He is not waiting around wondering what is going to happen next. He wants you to step out of the known and into the unknown. He wants you to step out of finite reasoning. Ephesians tells us that Jesus *"raised us up together"* (Ephesians 2:6). That means that when Jesus was raised from the dead, we were raised from the dead. Jesus didn't just suffer *for* you; He suffered *as* you. He didn't just die on the cross *for* you; He died on the cross *as* you. He was not only buried *for* you; He was buried *as* you. He not only descended into the heart of the earth *for* you; He descended into the heart of the earth *as* you. Likewise, on the third day, when the stone was rolled away, He rose again—and so did you!

Jesus didn't raise you up to hang out in a graveyard, but to be a vessel worthy of the manifestation of Ephesians 2:6—He *"raised us up together, and made us sit together in the heavenly places in Christ Jesus."* He gave you a spectacular view, according to His concept of time and reality—a seat in eternity where you can now have access to the present, past, and future. God's eternity cannot be measured by time. He stepped out of eternity and into time in order to free you from the constraints of time. Now, He gives you the privilege of eternity and the opportunity to sit down next to Him at the right hand of the Father in order to see things according to His concept of time and reality.

Our understanding is often shallow in comparison to what He has done for us and where He has placed us. I often wonder, regarding the writings of Paul, *Why did the apostle Paul write that he was moving beyond the foundational things that he had been preaching and begin to build on other things?* God showed me that it was because He continued to reveal Himself in greater measure to Paul so that we could have the Word that we live by today. The power and anointing of Christ resides inside of you. You are no longer in the graveyard. You are seated in heavenly places with Him, and you have an overall view that enables you to experience the coming age in advance.

By faith, you can have a glimpse of your destiny. Not with

natural eyes but with the eyes of God—according to the concept of time and reality that abides in His consciousness. The Lord has given us the ability to see our life through spiritual eyes, but too often our vision is obstructed by our natural surroundings. Know with all of your heart that God almighty has prepared things for you that you cannot comprehend with your finite, human, earth-based mind. Embrace the truth concerning God's reality with your spirit, and your flesh will follow suit.

AN ATTITUDE OF WORSHIP

I remember the first time someone told me, "If you give your life to Christ, right now you're going to be a new creature. You're going to have a new lease on life!" Something within me ignited when I heard those words. At that time, I was an alcoholic, and I was losing my family. I was a singer on the nightclub circuit, and everything in my life was falling apart. That's when God, in His timing and design, sent a preacher to me with some good news. "If you'll give your life to Jesus, He'll make you brand-new. He'll start you over." I said, "Oh God! That's exactly what I need right now." I didn't need money at that time; I just needed to start over. That day, I embraced God's promise without hesitation.

> THE LORD HAS GIVEN US THE ABILITY TO SEE OUR LIFE THROUGH SPIRITUAL EYES, BUT TOO OFTEN OUR VISION IS OBSTRUCTED BY OUR NATURAL SURROUNDINGS.

Embrace the fact that God's concept of time and reality is

moving on your behalf. Even though you can't see it, the Rock is moving for you. The Rock may look stationary, sitting at the right hand of the Father, but behind the scenes He is moving on your behalf. The new view you now have reveals the truth that God can work it all out and give you a fresh start. It may not always be a pleasant experience, but God will work it out on His side of reality, not yours.

> *And we know that all things work together for good to those who love God, to those who are the called according to His purpose.* (Romans 8:28)

You are here for a reason; there's no one else like you. You are so special that God went way out of His way to send His Son to deliver to you in His concept of time and reality. Purge the files of old data and download God's glory. He saw your faith when you were yet unformed.

> *For whatever is born of God overcomes the world. And this is the victory that has overcome the world; our faith.* (1 John 5:4)

Aligning yourself with God's concept of time and reality is absolutely necessary in order for you to press on toward the mark for the prize of His higher calling. If you don't adapt to God's mind-set, you may end up stagnated in a state of mediocrity, a state that hinders the life of many Christians.

So, worship God, not for what you can see in the natural, but for what you see Him doing behind the scenes in the Spirit. It is in that worship where God not only eases the pain, but He removes the source of the affliction. As you immerse yourself in an attitude of worship, He will cleanse you from all the heaviness that the enemy has placed upon you. As you worship Him, you become one with Him. Fear, torment, and affliction must flee in the presence of almighty God.

If you're reading this book and you've never accepted Jesus as your Lord and Savior, this can be your day. Jesus Himself said, *"I am the way, the truth, and the life. No one comes to the Father except through Me"* (John 14:6). Then, in Romans we are promised, *"If you confess with your mouth the Lord Jesus and believe in your heart that God has raised Him from the dead, you will be saved"* (Romans 10:9). If you would like to accept Jesus as your Lord and Savior, today is the perfect time. Open your heart to God. Receive the love that He has for you. Repent of your sins and leave them at the foot of the cross as we agree together in the following prayer:

Jesus, I repent for my sins.

I believe that You're my Savior.

I believe that You died and rose again in my behalf.

This day, I choose to follow You and be born again. Amen.

If you earnestly prayed that prayer with all your heart, then you are born again. It really is that simple. You're a Christian, a believer—welcome to the family of God!

Now you must find a good Bible-believing, Bible-teaching church that will help you to know your Savior better and to walk out your salvation. Remember to seek the Lord in all things for His timing and to allow the Lord Jesus to richly bless your life.

CHAPTER EIGHT

GOD'S KINGDOM OF INFINITE POSSIBILITIES

GOD'S KINGDOM OF INFINITE POSSIBILITIES

*Now to Him who is able to do exceedingly
abundantly above all that we ask or think,
according to the power that works in us.*
—Ephesians 3:20

As you learn to live your life based upon how God designed you, don't allow the subtle distractions of the tempter to steer you from your course of victory. When he comes to try you, maintain your spiritual stand, focusing on what God has said in His Word rather than on the devil's depiction of your capabilities.

After being baptized and affirmed as God's *"beloved Son"* (Matthew 3:17), Jesus was led by the Spirit into the wilderness to be tempted by the devil. As recorded in Matthew, after He'd fasted for forty days and nights, Jesus was hungry.

> *Now when the tempter came to Him, he said, "If You are the Son of God, command that these stones become bread."*
>
> (Matthew 4:3)

At your weakest moment, Satan will come to try your faith by tempting your fleshly desires. When he comes, despite your frailty, you must be as vigilant and alert as Jesus, knowing that *"the weapons of our warfare are not carnal but mighty in God for pulling down strongholds"* (2 Corinthians 10:4). It's a spiritual battle—a tug-of-war between spirit and flesh. Jesus was well aware of this bigger picture and, when tempted by the devil, responded with the Word of God:

> *It is written, "Man shall not live by bread alone, but by every word that proceeds from the mouth of God."*
>
> (Matthew 4:4)

Scripture diverts attention from our own needs and onto the deity of God. It's a constant reminder that we live by more than our own natural appetites. Rather, we live by *"every word that proceeds from the mouth of God."* The words that proceed out of God's mouth toward His children are a powerful means of spiritual nutrition for the believer's holistic well-being. You are living among God's infinite possibilities, and only you can prevent yourself from partaking of His many gifts.

INFINITE POSSIBILITIES

Reverend Dorise Vance received a mandate from God to establish a prayer center in Palm Springs, California. At the time, she had no funds, no staff, no plan, not to mention the fact that she was seventy-five years of age. Nevertheless, all these obstacles would not stop her. It wasn't all the things she didn't have that mattered. What mattered was the revelation that our God is able to do exceeding abundantly above all that we could ask or think. She had an uncommon ability to grasp the reality of God's kingdom of infinite possibilities.

To this day, her ministry is thriving with power and expectation, as she moves forward to accomplish and fulfill God's divine intention for her life.

RECEIVING GOD'S SIGNAL

When Jesus answered temptation by saying, *"Man shall not live by bread alone, but by every word that proceeds from the mouth of God,"* He was really saying, "You shouldn't be more concerned about physical food than you are about spiritual food—the Word of God." On Sunday mornings, there are some in the congregation who struggle to focus on the message being preached because they're thinking about what to have for lunch or dinner following the service. This concern about physical food is a part of human nature. But the Lord says, "Put that particular need in second place." Although we need physical nourishment, before indulging in natural replenishment you need to first make time to consume your spiritual food.

As a pastor, many have come to me in desperation as they struggle to find direction for their lives. I often use the illustration of a satellite dish being installed. In North America, they must be pointed in the right direction, the south sky, in order to receive the signal from a satellite positioned in the heavenlies. It is no different for us. We too must be pointed in the right direction. The question then arises: how do we accomplish this?

ABIDE IN THE WORD

First of all, we must continue to *abide* in God's Word. But the Word you continue in is not only the Word you read, memorize, and quote. In John, Jesus said, *"If you abide in My word, you are My disciples indeed. And you shall know the truth, and the truth shall make you free"* (John 8:31–32). The key words here are *if* and *and.* It is a conditional sentence. *If* you continue in My Word, at that time you will be My disciple, you will begin to know the truth, *and* that truth will make you free and keep you free. It's not just abiding in the Word and it's not just reading and memorizing Scripture. It's the Word, of God that you choose to *live* that ultimately leads to freedom. If God's Word is not vibrantly alive within you, it is difficult to find your way.

> IT'S THE WORD OF GOD THAT YOU *CHOOSE* TO LIVE THAT ULTIMATELY LEADS TO FREEDOM.

One day, many years ago, I had been studying the Word for many hours, preparing for a message. Suddenly, the Spirit of the Lord spoke to my heart, saying, "I want you to spend quality time in My Word." I answered, defensively, "What do You mean, Lord? I've been studying for hours." He then revealed to me that, although I'd been studying, what He wanted was intimate quality time to commune with me through His Word.

A LIFESTYLE OF PRAYER

The second step is to adopt a lifestyle of prayer. Most of us pray diligently when we need something. But prayer supersedes the realm of petition and encompasses every aspect of life.

In 1 Kings 10, we are told that the queen of Sheba made a long and difficult journey so that she might speak to King Solomon about all the questions in her heart, for she had heard of the fame of his wisdom. We have a source of wisdom that is greater than Solomon. Jesus is wisdom incarnate. Unfortunately, many of us are more than willing to discuss the difficulties of our journey with others but are far too silent with Him.

> GOD'S DESIGN FOR YOUR LIFE FAR SURPASSES ANYTHING YOU COULD EVER IMAGINE OR DREAM FOR YOURSELF.

Continue in God's Word, saturating and expanding your consciousness, because a mind that has been expanded with the Word of God will never return to its original shape. Then, as you move forward in faith, do it prayerfully, acknowledging Him in all your ways that He might direct your path. (See Proverbs 3:6.)

God's Word is the foundation for your success. God's Word is inerrant, immutable, and infallible. It cannot fail or return void. It is perfection and does not pass away. It will meet your every need. The answer may not always appear on the surface; you may have to dig deep into His Word to find the solution to your particular situation. But as you do, you will find everything that you need to absolutely succeed in your endeavors.

No matter the stories you've heard, no matter what society presents to you, you are here on a divine assignment. God's design for your life far surpasses anything you could ever imagine or dream for yourself. In fact, if you knew the fullness that God desires for your life, you would probably be amazed and think it impossible. Once again, that's why Jesus said, *"If you can believe, all things are possible to him who believes"* (Mark 9:23).

GREATNESS LIVES WITHIN

Do you not know that you are the temple of God and that the Spirit of God dwells in you? (1 Corinthians 3:16)

The very same Spirit that raised Christ from the dead on resurrection Sunday is dwelling inside of you. The same Spirit that hovered over the waters in the beginning when the earth was void of form and God said, *"Let there be light,"* is the same Spirit that abides in you. (See Genesis 1:2–3.) You are the house of God, and the Spirit of God dwells in you. *"But the anointing which you have received from Him abides in you"* (1 John 2:27).

You are of God and have overcome the world because *"He who is in you is greater than he who is in the world"* (1 John 4:4). Greater is He than sickness and disease. Greater is He than sin, addiction, or any other temptation. Greater is He that is in you than any adversity that the enemy may hurl your way. Despite lack of confidence, financial struggles, and challenges, God has designed and equipped you to overcome such challenges.

Do you not know that you are the temple of God and that the Spirit of God dwells in you? If anyone defiles the temple of God, God will destroy him. For the temple of God is holy, which temple you are. Let no one deceive himself. If anyone among you seems to be wise in this age, let him become a fool that he may become wise. For the wisdom of this world is foolishness with God. For it is written, "He catches the wise in their own craftiness"; and again, "The LORD knows the thoughts of the wise, that they are futile."

(1 Corinthians 3:16–20)

POWER OF INNOCENCE

In Mark 10, we find an account of Jesus teaching and preaching the Word of God and ministering to the needs of those who were present. He operated with such power that some of the people began to bring their children to Him, wanting Him to pray for them and lay His hands on them. When the disciples saw that they were bringing children to Jesus, they rebuked the parents, saying, in effect, "Don't let these kids bother the Lord...He's ministering!" But when Jesus heard this, He was very displeased, and said,

Let the little children come to Me, and do not forbid them; for of such is the kingdom of God....Whoever does not receive the kingdom of God as a little child will by no means enter it. (Mark 10:14–15)

Children are very receptive to the Word of God. Perhaps it's because children already have a mind-set that is open to endless possibilities. When a baby enters this world, in his own mind there is nothing he can't do. Babies are fearless, because to them, all things are possible. We call this innocence or naiveté. Hence, "for their own good" we begin to teach babies fear and tell them what is and is not possible. We tell the baby what can be accomplished and what can't be accomplished. We teach the child about all of the things that could possibly harm them. We pass on to them our own accomplishments and our own failures. We program them according to our experiences. Too often, children grow up without being taught who they truly are and how to develop their own unique character.

In teaching the child who we are, he or she takes up where we left off. We produce a replica of ourselves. In this way, we were all molded and shaped by the good and bad ideologies of others. The irony is that we spend the rest of our lives trying to recover what we originally had when we first entered the world. We may search for a lifetime, looking for something that has always been there.

When Moses delivered God's people from the bondage of Egypt, he delivered them with many miraculous signs and wonders. They left Egypt with wealth, and there was not a feeble or sick one among them. It was not like what we see in the movie *The Ten Commandments* where the people were frail and barely had strength to travel. They were not struggling and sick. The Bible says that Moses *"brought them out with silver and gold, and there was none feeble among His tribes"* (Psalm 105:37). They left with all the health and wealth of Egypt, with signs and wonders going before them.

When they got to the Red Sea and heard Pharaoh's chariot wheels in hot pursuit, Moses commanded the children of Israel, *"Stand still, and see the salvation of the LORD"* (Exodus 14:13). Then Moses raised his rod, the sea parted before them, and they walked across on dry land. When they were safely on the other side, Moses lowered his rod, and the sea caved in on Pharaoh's army, who were seen never again. (See Exodus 14:16–28.)

The children of Israel were delivered from bondage with great and miraculous power; yet, as they proceeded to make their way to the land of promise, it took them forty years to make an eleven-day journey. Because of their unbelief, they kept going around the same old desert year after year, searching for something that was always there.

I can't help but feel that this is the picture of the body of Christ today. So often we keep going around in circles, in essence, taking forty years to make an eleven-day journey. We keep passing by what is already there on our behalf. God has prepared wonders and blessing and purpose for us since the foundation of the world, but we can't see it due to our fear, lack of perception, and unbelief.

UNDISCOVERED TREASURES

Everywhere Jesus went, He preached about the presence of the kingdom. *"The time is fulfilled, and the kingdom of God is at hand"* (Mark 1:15). He preached this message so much that in Luke the Pharisees demanded to know when the kingdom of God would come. Jesus answered, *"The kingdom of God does not come with observation....For indeed, the kingdom of God is within you"* (Luke 17:20–21). You can't see it coming because it dwells within. The kingdom of God is already here with us.

Jesus prepared the kingdom for us from the foundation of the world. Therefore, everything that we need to accomplish our divine purpose and destiny is here. And since the kingdom is within us, we don't have to look in outer space for the undiscovered treasures that the Lord has prepared for us. It's in "inner space." God's kingdom is within you, and anything that threatens your quest to discover it will have to fall away.

In Ephesians 3:20, Paul was desperate to communicate the depth of God's infinite possibilities, *"Now to Him who is able to do exceedingly abundantly above all that we ask or think, according to the power that works in us."* It's all according to the power— God's power that resides within us. The devil is no match for God's power in you. *"And these signs will follow those who believe: in My name they will cast out demons"* (Mark 16:17). You have the power to command the devil to loose his grip and cast him out into the desert places.

Each of us are involved in a journey, a journey that can become rough, but it's only part of the process of becoming who you already are by following God's design. Along the path, the enemy may throw obstacles at you to hinder your progress. If he can discourage you by making you sick, he'll attack your health. If he can discourage you by giving you financial challenges, he will uproot your economical stability. If he can distract you by attacking your marriage, he'll do that. He'll try whatever it takes to keep you from reaching your destination. You may begin to question the direction in which you're headed:

- *"Where is God in all of this?"*
- *"Am I the only one going through rough times?"*
- *"I've been praying, going to church, practicing forgiveness, and tithing, but where is God?"*

God is not in your circumstances or your situation. He is in you! But it is up to you to invoke that power and authority upon your situation in order to experience victory, knowing that God is working through you to overcome the challenges of the world.

YOU ARE NOT ALONE

When you pass through the waters, I will be with you; and through the rivers, they shall not overflow you. When you walk through the fire, you shall not be burned, nor shall the flame scorch you. (Isaiah 43:2)

God is always with you. He'll never leave you or forsake you. (See Hebrews 13:5.) But He's not in the water or the fire; He's in you. No matter how bad your plight appears to be in the natural, know that you serve a God who will always provide a way of escape.

GOD IS NOT IN YOUR CIRCUMSTANCES OR YOUR SITUATION. HE IS IN YOU!

While we do not look at the things which are seen, but at the things which are not seen. For the things which are seen are temporary, but the things which are not seen are eternal. (2 Corinthians 4:18)

What you currently see taking place in your life is temporal; but, behind the scenes in the eternal eyes of God, He has already provided for your victory. With your natural eyes, you can't always see the handiwork of God, which is why uncompromising faith is so pertinent to the believer's life. The minute you receive the revelation that there is something beyond what can be seen, the door will open to God's infinite possibilities.

"'My thoughts are not your thoughts, nor are your ways My ways,' says the Lord" (Isaiah 55:8). Renew your mind according to His Word. In doing so, during times of trouble, you can access higher levels of thinking in the decision-making realm of your renewed mind and allow the power and anointing of God that resides within to deliver you from the snares of the enemy and forewarn you of oncoming danger.

Spiritual Vision

In 2 Kings, we find another account of Elisha, who kept warning Israel every time Syria was about to attack so they would be prepared. Finally, the king of Syria decided to call a meeting with his servants to find out who was betraying him by warning the Israelites. He said, *"Will you not show me which of us is for the king of Israel?"* (2 Kings 6:11). Then one of his men spoke up, *"None, my lord, O king; but Elisha, the prophet who is in Israel, tells the king of Israel the words that you speak in your bedroom"* (verse 12). That got the King's attention. He decided that something had to be done about Elisha.

"Go and see where he is, that I may send and get him." And it was told him, saying, "Surely he is in Dothan." (verse 13)

So he sent chariots and armed men, a mighty army, to go recover this one man because he wanted to put this problem out of commission. That led to Elisha praying for his servant's eyes to be opened in order to see the great heavenly army protecting them. (See 2 Kings 6:17.)

You too need spiritual vision to see the hand of God and the unseen, spiritual world. Step into another dimension of the Lord your God and put the devil under your feet, realizing that you have the kingdom of infinite possibilities dwelling inside of you. When you begin to walk in the kingdom of infinite possibilities, you will realize, not with mental assent but according to God's Word, that you can't lose. You might be knocked down, but you won't be knocked out.

But once again, the destiny that God has designed for you is something you must choose. The decision to rise up is one that only you can make.

The Lord wants to remove every doubt and every fear. He wants you to realize that you're standing in the very power and authority of the resurrected Christ, and that you're a resurrected life in progress. At this very moment, God's infinite possibilities are within you, enabling you to put all adversity under your feet and move toward your destiny in the anointing, power, and guidance of the Lord Jesus Christ. Even when the enemy attacks your health and your mind, you must remember that God's kingdom of infinite possibilities is bigger than cancer, bigger than tumors, bigger than anything that the enemy may throw at you.

> THE DESTINY THAT GOD HAS DESIGNED FOR YOU IS SOMETHING YOU MUST CHOOSE.

Healing is also a part of the covenant. When the doctors shake their heads and say, "There is nothing more we can do," keep your mind focused on the divine Healer of all things. When all else fails, the power of God within you will rise up and devour cancer and disease. When you come out of traumatic trials of sickness and mental anguish, you will grow stronger because God is faithful to remove the threat of the devourer and silence his roar.

> *Bless the Lord, O my soul, and forget not all His benefits who forgives all your iniquities, who heals all your diseases, who redeems your life from destruction, who crowns you with lovingkindness and tender mercies.* (Psalm 103:2–4)

Know that the power that works in you is the power of God, and it enables you to overcome all the tactics of the enemy and enter your door of endless possibilities through Christ Jesus. The Word of God, which He has written on your behalf before the foundation of the world, continues to stand firm today. Are you ready to begin seeing the manifestation of what God has written and designed on your behalf? Then let us agree together in the following prayer:

> *Father, Your Word declares that before the foundation of the world You knew me. My prayer is that Your will would be done in my life and that You would give me spiritual insight to see myself as You see me. I pray that the manifestation of Your anointing will be realized in my life and that my steps will be ordered by Your Spirit. Guide me and lead me into all truth, that my days shall be prosperous, and that the favor of the Lord may reign and rule my days ahead. Thank You that my faith has been renewed. I decree and declare that with You, all things are possible, and that I shall witness the full manifestation of all the things that You have designed on my behalf, according to Your power. In Jesus' name. Amen.*

Every word of God is pure; He is a shield to those who put their trust in Him. (Proverbs 30:5)

About the Author

ABOUT THE AUTHOR

D anny Diaz is the founder and senior pastor of Victorious Living Christian Center in Pomona, California. His ministry has a global sphere of influence through his international television program, *Victorious Revelation with Pastor Danny Diaz*, which is seen and heard throughout the world, affording him the opportunity to impact the lives of so many in their time of need.

Pastor Danny Diaz has the heart of an apostle and is much sought after as a speaker who brings forth an insightful view of God's concept of time and reality and his intention for our lives in the now of the times. Danny and his wife, Yolanda, have two children and two grandchildren.

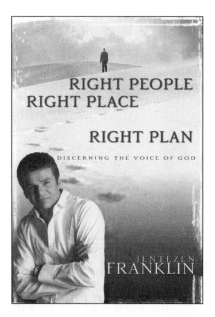

Right People, Right Place, Right Plan:
Discerning the Voice of God
Jentezen Franklin

Whom should I marry? What will I do with my life?
Do I take this job? Should I invest money in this opportunity?

God has bestowed an incredible gift in the heart of every believer.
He has given you an internal compass to help guide your life, your
family, your children, your finances, and much more. Jentezen Franklin
reveals how, through the Holy Spirit, you can tap into the heart
and mind of the Almighty. Learn to trust those divine "nudges" and
separate God's voice from all other voices in your life. Tap into your
supernatural gift of spiritual discernment and you will better be able
to fulfill your purpose as a child of God.

ISBN: 978-0-88368-276-0 • Hardcover • 208 pages

WHITAKER
HOUSE

www.whitakerhouse.com

The Most Important Person on Earth:
The Holy Spirit, Governor of the Kingdom

Dr. Myles Munroe

In *The Most Important Person on Earth*, Dr. Myles Munroe explains
how the Holy Spirit is the Governor of God's kingdom on earth,
much as royal governors administered the will of earthly kings
in their territories. Under the guidance and enabling of the Holy
Spirit, you will discover how to bring order to the chaos in your life,
receive God's power to heal and deliver, fulfill your true purpose
with joy, become a leader in your sphere of influence, and be part of
God's government on earth. Enter into the fullness of God's Spirit
as you embrace God's design for your life today.

ISBN: 978-0-88368-986-8 • Hardcover • 320 pages

www.whitakerhouse.com

**Freedom to Forget:
Releasing Pain from the Past,
Embracing Hope for the Future**
Dan Willis

Anger…Bitterness…Depression…
How can we move forward when tormenting memories of past
hurts constantly consume us? Through humor and personal
anecdotes, Dan Willis shows the way to complete forgiveness and
healing. Discover how you can forgive those who have hurt you,
overcome family dysfunction, break free from resulting destructive
behaviors, and begin to walk in a life of blessings and peace.
Experience such a deep healing that you will be able to forget the
pain of the past, escape the bondage that has held you hostage,
and move on to enjoy your God-given freedom!

ISBN: 978-0-88368-222-7 • Trade • 208 pages

WHITAKER
HOUSE

www.whitakerhouse.com

Anointing for Healing
Melanie Hemry & Gina Lynnes

Melanie Hemry and Gina Lynnes share personal experiences and researched testimonies of people miraculously healed by a powerful God who still works in our lives today. Even when the situation was seemingly hopeless, God intervened to heal. This combination of amazing stories and powerful Scripture will have you in awe and wonder over the greatness and love of God. You will learn the significance of anointing oil when praying for healing, discover how to pray effectively, and find inspiration for your Christian walk. This book is what you need to break through to your healing experience.

ISBN: 978-0-88368-687-4 • Gift • 176 pages

Anointing for Children
Melanie Hemry & Gina Lynnes

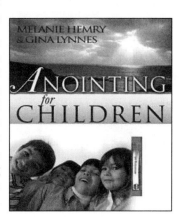

The devil is out to get our children. Most of us have already figured that out. What we need to know is how to keep them out of his hands. Find out how other determined parents have done it. Discover the scriptural truths that inspired them and witness the miracles that happened in their children's lives as they stepped out in faith on God's Word. Whether you're hoping to have a baby, needing healing for your child, or praying for a prodigal to come home, *Anointing for Children* has a message of hope and faith for you.

ISBN: 978-0-88368-686-7 • Gift • 192 pages

WHITAKER
HOUSE

www.whitakerhouse.com

Anointing for Protection
Melanie Hemry & Gina Lynnes

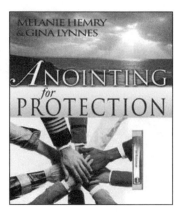

God has the power to protect His people from danger. Eloise Wright proved it in a Dallas parking lot when a kidnapper locked her at gunpoint in the trunk of her car. Eloise's astounding story, along with the testimonies of other believers who faced hair-raising disasters in faith and miraculously survived them unharmed, are a thrilling reminder that the God of the Bible is still guarding His people today. Find out how you can build your life on God's promises of protection so that you too can live in supernatural security even in the most dangerous of times.

ISBN: 978-0-88368-689-8 • Gift • 208 pages

Anointing for Loved Ones' Salvation
Melanie Hemry & Gina Lynnes

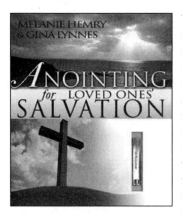

Some people need a Damascus road experience—a supernatural manifestation of the Holy Spirit, a sign or a wonder like those in the book of Acts—to bring them out of darkness and into the light. But do such things still happen today? Absolutely. These thrilling stories prove it. Full of real-life testimonies told by those who have been dramatically saved, this book abounds with clear, scriptural promises that will inspire you to pray for lost loved ones with fresh fervor and faith. It will help keep you on your knees until the victory is won.

ISBN: 978-0-88368-688-1 • Gift • 192 pages

www.whitakerhouse.com